THROUGH A
GLASS DARKLY—
BUT I STILL SEE!

Reflections of a Believing Thinker and a Thinking Believer

Through A Glass Darkly—But I Still See! Reflections of a
Believing Thinker and a Thinking Believer
Published by Rusty Gates Books, L.L.C.
145 Queen Road
Lawndale, NC 28090
Copyright © D. Larry Gregg 2005

Library of Congress Cataloging-in-Publication Data

ISBN 1-893330-43-5

Gregg, D. Larry, Through a Glass Darkly—But I Still See!
Reflections of a Believing Thinker and a Thinking Believer
1. Collection of Reflective Essays—2. Religious Meditations—3.
Theological Reflections—4. Exercises in Critical Thinking—5.
Apologetics.

Published by Rusty Gates Books, L.L.C. 145 Queen Road,
Lawndale, NC 28090. Telephone (704) 538-7900. E-mail
Wisewms@bellsouth.net.
Printed in the United States of America
10 9 8 7 6 5 4 3 2 1

THROUGH A GLASS DARKLY—

BUT I STILL SEE!

Reflections of a Believing Thinker and a Thinking Believer

D. LARRY GREGG, PhD

Rusty Gates Books, L.L.C.
145 Queen Road
Lawndale, NC 28090

Dedication

To Peggy, beloved wife, through whom everything significant in my life has been achieved.

THROUGH A GLASS DARKLY, BUT I STILL SEE!

Reflections of a Believing Thinker
and a Thinking Believer

CONTENTS

INTRODUCTION

The contemporary market is replete with volumes of Christian literature. Why then would I wish to write another one? The reason is that much of what I see focuses upon inspiration, and the creation of "warm fuzzy" feelings of acceptance and intimacy with God, or upon luridly fanciful speculation regarding the Second Coming and the end of the world. While there is an appropriate place for such books, it seems to me there is also a profound need for works that challenge the reader to think carefully about a life lived in appropriate relationship to God, and to others. This particular little volume is aimed at ministering to the needs of *believing thinkers* and *thinking believers*.

Through a Glass Darkly, But I Still See! aims to stimulate critical reflection on the part of the reader by taking seriously the injunction to "love the Lord, your God with all your *heart*, and with all your *mind* . . ." (Mt. 22:37). Its basic premise is that, to piggyback on Socrates, "The unexamined *faith* is not worth having."

For more than thirty years this writer has been intimately involved in the ongoing life of the Christian community as believer, vocational minister, theological educator, and writer. Over the decades I have attempted to think seriously about my beliefs as a Christian, through the various lenses of my professional experience and training. Thus I write, not only as trained theologian and academician, but as husband/father, the caregiver of an invalid parent, pastor/teacher, neighbor, and friend.

Through a Glass Darkly, But I Still See! consists of a collection of reflections/commentaries that touch upon many of the questions with which thinking believers often struggle. I make no promise to offer neatly packaged answers or solutions. Rather, I will attempt to wrestle honestly with the topics and, in doing so, help the reader hone the skills necessary to do his/her own believing reflection. My intent is to offer hope to those who struggle, but don't always arrive at a clear solution; to challenge the prideful complacency of those who are sure they know all the answers, when they haven't yet discovered all the questions; to think believingly as a believing thinker with others who, while they don't "get it" all the time, do think they understand some things.

The genesis of these reflections is rooted in the decision, during the summer of 1997, to begin writing brief essays for submission to various Christian publications. Subsequently some of these pieces have been seen in formats such as *Mature Years*, a publication of the United Methodist Church, and *America*, a Roman Catholic publication. In the spring of 2004, Calvary Baptist Church in Rutherfordton, NC began a Sunday morning radio program, and the essays featured in this volume became the basis of my morning messages in that format. Printed copies of the essays were made available for parishioners to pick up following the weekly broadcasts. Many suggested that a collection of the essays would make a useful tool for Christian devotional reflection and thoughtful discussion.

Obviously there are many people who contribute to the development of a work such as this. While I cannot express gratitude to all in this place, there are some who must not remain unacknowledged. First, there is Peggy Gregg, my wife of thirty-five years, whose willingness to share the joys and trials of life with me is the greatest blessing of my existence. Only through her encouragement and love am I able, by God's grace, to accomplish anything useful and worthwhile.

My professional colleague, and the Dean of Arts and Sciences at Isothermal Community College, Dr. Nancy Womack, graciously read and made notations regarding the essays. Her capacity to look through a lens different from mine has been invaluable in clarifying my thinking on various topics.

Mrs. Helen Roach, dear friend for many years, patiently read each essay and offered suggestions regarding structure and style.

And finally, there are the people of Calvary Baptist Church. I find great delight in serving as their pastor. It is a joy to share together with them in bearing witness to the Christian faith.

CHAPTER ONE
Through a Glass Darkly, But I Still See

We live in a time of radical absolutes. Whether one listens to political leaders, social analysts, economic gurus, entertainment personalities, technology experts, or religious figures, many discussions focus on opposites. It is either the best of times, or it's the worst of times. Great strides are being made in harmonious human relationships, or human beings are regressing into barbaric tribalism. Economic prosperity is within reach of everyone, or the entire global economy is on the brink of catastrophic collapse. This dramatic difference of opinion is nowhere more apparent than when one listens to, or attempts to participate in, discussions concerning religious faith. On the one hand, there are those who are absolutely certain they have cornered the market on religious truth. It is necessary only to listen to them, and do their bidding, to know the perfect will of God. On the other hand, there are those who are equally sure all religion is no more than the by-product of human striving to make some sense out of an inexplicable, and probably meaningless, existence. From their perspective, one religious insight or point of view is about as good as another and, while religion, properly managed, may have some measure of personal and social value, any talk of genuinely knowing and being known by God is no more than delusion and wish-fulfillment.

The truth is that this whole business of understanding God is filled with mystery. I must confess, I don't think I get it all the time. Yet, in the same breath, I'm compelled to assert that I think I do get it some of the time. Further, I think I gradually get more and more of it if I make a conscious, honest effort to get it. But sometimes I discover that even though I thought I had gotten it; I hadn't. And, conversely, I discover that sometimes I've gotten more of it than I thought I had. While some people appear to be getting it better than I do, I'm not sure all these people are getting it as fully as they would like for me to think. And, finally, I'm sure that those who profess to have gotten all of it are just blowing smoke.

By now you're wondering, "Is this idiot going somewhere, or is he just rambling on with no clear idea of where he is going?" The answer is, "Yes! Yes, I am going somewhere." And "Yes, I am not absolutely sure where I'm going." However, I'm convinced that I'm in good company along the way. The Apostle Paul understood that much spiritual reality is shrouded in the mystery of the radical distinction between God and humanity: God is God and you and I are not. Thus, while not avoiding the responsibility of striving to grow in insight and understanding, Paul willingly conceded "for now we see through a glass, darkly, but then face to face; now I know in part; but then I shall know even as also I am known" (I Cor. 13:12 KJV). Paul's simile is that of seeing one's reflection in the polished glass, or brass, or stone that was the ancient equivalent of the modern mirror. Lacking the reflective qualities of modern mirrors, these antique "looking glasses" were unable to reflect an image with photographic clarity. However, while the image was oftentimes distorted, it still reflected a relatively faithful and recognizable image of the original.

In Genesis 1:26 we are told that human beings are created in the *image* and *likeness* of God, their Creator. In Genesis 3 we are told of the tragic consequences of human sinfulness expressed in the desire to be "as gods" ourselves, rather than remaining content with reflecting God's image. Theologians, Jewish, Christian, and Islamic, have struggled mightily with the implication of human fallenness for the divine image in our personhood. Some have argued that the image has been irretrievably lost and that human beings, by nature, no longer reflect God's image. Others hold that, though marred, out-of-focus, and distorted, the image of God is inherent to the nature of human personhood. To be human is to reflect, in some limited measure, the reality of God.

From childhood I have been plagued by astigmatism. This visual difficulty is defined as "the defect of an eye or of a lens that makes objects look indistinct or gives imperfect images" (*The World Book Dictionary*, 1971 ed., "Astigmatism"). This irregularity in the shape of the eyeball is accompanied by nearsightedness. Close objects are distinct without aid, but those at a distance are mere blurs. I have always been able to identify with the man Jesus met who said he could "see men as trees, walking" (Mk. 8:24).

While this problem has been troublesome, it is nothing compared with the difficulty experienced by those who are totally blind. Without the aid of corrective lenses what I see is often fuzzy, out of focus, indistinct, and imperfect. Sometimes it is "Through a Glass Darkly," yet "I Still See!" And this is precisely my point. I don't see everything, but I do see some things. I don't get everything, but I do get some things. I don't know everything, but I do understand some things. And, while I can never see it all, get it all, or know it all; with the appropriate help, I can see, get, and know more and more with the passage of time.

I tell the college students I teach that *epistemology* is the fancy philosophical word for questions related to what we can know and how we know what we know. Since Plato many have argued that we are born with an instinctive awareness of some things or, to use a modern analogy, we come into existence with some programming already loaded on our hard drives. The disciples of John Locke assert that at birth the human mind is a blank slate. From this perspective all that is contained in human consciousness is the product of sensory experience and our subsequent thinking about those experiences. Put more simply, Platonic idealists argue that we know what we know from the inside out. Locke's followers argue that we know what we know from the outside in.

One of my former teachers often spoke of the differences between analytic and synthetic reasoning (Eric C. Rust, *Religion, Revelation, and Reason*, Macon, GA: Mercer University Press, 1981, pp. 101-109). By analytic thinking he meant the process of examining reality piece by piece. This approach to reasoning makes use of the tools of modern scientific method. It weights, measures, compares, and describes. Synthetic reasoning is less concerned with the examination of individual pieces of reality. This approach is concerned with wholes and with how integrated wholes are always more than the sum of the various pieces and parts.

It may be that much of the human tendency toward radically opposing viewpoints is the product of the fact that some of us, on the basis of no more than how our brains are wired, have a greater affinity for the analytic approach, while others tend to favor the synthetic, integrative approach to looking at life. If this is true, we need to be careful about heavy-handed assertions that "my way is better than your way." In reality, it may simply be true that "my way is my way," and "your way is your way." Further, it probably is true that the most effective method for arriving at any kind of truth, including religious truth, involves the appropriate use of both these approaches. To use a droll illustration, I can use the tools of science to describe a kiss, but anyone who has ever been kissed knows there is more involved than just science.

I have five lenses through which I may acquire information, knowledge, and understanding. They are the lenses of scientific observation, rational reflection, instinctive reaction, emotional response, and divine revelation. However, further reflection suggests that lying behind each of these lenses is a basic assumption of faith. By faith, scientific observation assumes that my senses (taste, touch, hearing, sight, and smell) are reporting to me accurate, reliable information. Rational reflection depends on the faith assumption of the truth of the presuppositions providing the logical foundation for my reflection. Instinctive reaction relies upon the faith assumption that the stimuli that trigger my instincts are actually what my subconscious mind assumes them to be. Emotional responses rest upon the faith assumption that I am emotionally balanced and in relatively good mental health. And the knowledge content in divine revelation assumes, by faith, that there is One other than myself who is infinitely greater than I and Who chooses to reveal Himself to me, and to others as well.

If these observations are true, then it may be argued that the overarching method of knowing, lying behind these diverse particular ways of knowing, is faith. At the ground of human consciousness, it is by faith that we know what we know, and it is by faith that we know we are known. And it is with these lenses that "through a glass darkly" we see and know all that we see and know.

All of the above suggests that, as a Christian believing thinker and thinking believer, I am called upon to affirm two basic insights. First, I have nothing to be ashamed of or embarrassed about as I profess to be a person of Christian faith, for all our knowledge is based upon certain faith assumptions. The faith assumption that a good and loving God has elected to reveal Himself, in history, the Bible, and most fully and completely in Jesus Christ, is no less sensible and worthy to be taken seriously than any other faith assumption.

Second, I am compelled to acknowledge that, while divine revelation is not arbitrary and irrational, God's revelation is made known to us through both non-rational and rational ways of knowing. This means that I am under obligation to take seriously the findings of modern scientific research, as well as the content of divine revelation. As a person of Christian faith, I am convinced that all authentic truth, wherever and however it is found, is ultimately and finally God's truth. And if all truth is ultimately God's truth, then we have nothing to fear in the truth.

My dear friends, faith and reason are not the opposites of one another. *Reasonable faith* and *faith-filled reason* are necessary tools for those who, though they see through a glass darkly, wish to grow in their understanding of God's will and purpose for His creation, and their role in that divine purpose. While we often must peer "through a glass, darkly," let's never give up on the truth that, because we are created in the image and likeness of God, we do have the capacity to see.

CHAPTER TWO
Believing Thinkers and Thinking Believers:
One is Not an Ox, and the Other is Not a Moron

The idea is at least as old as Augustine of Hippo, for he wrote, "... no one believes anything unless he has first thought that it is to be believed. It is not everyone who thinks that believes, since many think in order that they may not believe; *but everybody who believes, thinks, — both thinks in believing, and believes in thinking"* (Augustine, *On the Predestination of the Saints*, The Nicene and Post-Nicene Fathers, ed. Philip Schaff, First Series, vol. 5, (Grand Rapids, MI: Eerdmans, 1956, p. 499). (Italics mine). In this passage this great early Christian theologian and pastor affirmed a dynamic relationship between "believing" and "thinking" in the Christian faith.

By definition an "oxymoron" consists of two concepts juxtaposed in such a way that they appear to constitute a contradiction in terms. We frequently make "wisecracks" about "military intelligence," "honest lawyers," "truthful politicians," and even "moral ministers" to illustrate the point, often without recognizing the oxymoronic nature of a "wisecrack" itself. We know that such generalizations are not absolutely true, but, on the other hand, we have experienced enough military blunders, dishonest lawyers, lying politicians, and immoral ministers to make us hesitant to trust any of them without question.

Across the ages there have been those, both within and outside the Christian community, who have denied the reality of any relation between faith affirmations and critical thinking. Such persons assert, directly or indirectly, that such phrases as "believing thinker" and "thinking believer" are oxymoronic in nature. Such attitudes deny the fruitfulness of meaningful dialogue between deeply held religious beliefs and critical reflective thinking. One is led to conclude that "If one thinks carefully one will cease to believe" or "If one believes strongly enough, careful thought is not necessary."

In the title of this piece I have chosen to assert, in "wisecrack" fashion, "Believing Thinkers and Thinking Believers: One is Not an Ox, and the Other is Not a Moron." While I am playing with the words a bit, there is a point I wish to make. Too often we contemptuously dismiss those who hold positions about politics, social issues, and religious values that differ from our own. Frequently we conclude that their disagreement with us is the consequence of ox-like stubbornness, moronic stupidity, or some combination of the two. Obviously this is both unfair and counter-productive. To equate my fixed opinions with high integrity, while viewing yours as the product of narrow-minded stubbornness; or to view agreement with me as a sign of intelligence, and disagreement with me as evidence of a lack of mental ability on your part, does both you and me a disservice. I am denied the potential corrective insight that emerges from having my ideas refined in the arena of public discussion. And you are denied the opportunity to contribute insight and experience from your own unique point of view. We are both diminished in personhood; one is silenced while the other shouts. Both are denied the opportunity to experience the fullness of insight that can be the product of our reflective collaboration. It is important that every responsible Christian be both a "believing thinker" and a "thinking believer." Careful thought and profound belief are not opposed to one another; rather they are two sides of the same coin. Augustine is correct, "everybody who believes thinks . . . ."

During my years as a teacher of undergraduate religion majors and seminary/divinity school students, I often observed, "I don't believe nearly as much as I did when I first became a Christian." The statement was phrased in this fashion, to some degree, for its shock value. Impressionable students were often scandalized and moved immediately to the conclusion that I was one of "those" professors who really didn't believe in God, or Jesus, or the Church. I would move on to explain that, as a young and less mature Christian, I lacked the critical tools to separate the central kernel of Christian faith and practice from the social, cultural, and habitual trappings that often were attached to it. And so my early belief system included false assumptions, prejudices, cultural idiosyncrasies, and the byproducts of misinformation and ignorance. Over the years much of this has been laid aside as I learned to discriminate better between what the Bible actually teaches about certain things, and what some people (myself included) often thought or wished it taught.

Frequently this has been a painful process for many reasons: Sometimes I preferred my original understanding because I was comfortable with it and the truth challenged my complacency, and demanded adjustments in my behavior. On other occasions my change of mind put me at odds with persons whom I respected because it placed me in disagreement with them. At still other times such refinements of my belief system required the public admission that I had been wrong earlier, and no one really likes to admit that he or she is wrong. Even worse, sometimes it required that I apologize and make amends to another who was injured by my insistence upon an inadequate understanding of Christian truth. The only thing most of us like less than admitting we are wrong is apologizing for the damage we have done. And so, often it is easier to stoutly defend an inadequate point of view than to acknowledge that our original position is unsupportable. We are like the story of the old preacher whose son was going through his sermon notes shortly after the father's death. In the margin of one not very well developed thought, the old man had written, "Argument weak here; yell like heck!" Likewise, we often seek to overcome the limitations of our long cherished opinions by "yelling like heck" when any voice is raised to the contrary. In human relationships the end result, if I may be permitted to change metaphors, is an increase in heat without any corresponding increase in light.

Today many seem to think they are caught between "the rock and the hard place" of two mutually exclusive and inflexible positions. Either one must check one's brain at the door of the church, and blindly embrace a body of predetermined, and often at best muddled and at worst contradictory, faith assertions. Or, for the sake of mental health and intellectual integrity, one must abandon all religious belief as nothing more than naïve superstition or neurotic dependence. Put more simply, many labor under the assumption that they have only two choices. Either they must believe everything and question nothing; or they must question everything and believe nothing. Surely there is a better alternative.

Perhaps this is an appropriate place to return to Augustine. In the selection quoted earlier, this great Christian personality asserted, ". . . everybody who believes, thinks, — both thinks in believing, and believes in thinking . . . ." Augustine envisioned a dynamic relationship between faith and reason in which faith takes precedence over reason, but faith does not outstrip reason by much. Thus Augustine's initial *Credo* (I believe) is a choice to suspend disbelief, at least for a time, in order that one may carefully examine the content of one's beliefs. It is a foundational assumption, on Augustine's part, that it is better to begin with "something" than with "nothing."

Here Augustine stands in the stream of thought that stems from Plato, who argued that ultimate reality is understood from the inside out (deductively), rather than from the outside in (inductively). The first approach begins by believing that "something" is true, and then uses rational reflection to explore the validity of the "something" believed. The second approach begins by believing that "nothing" is true and, through scientific observation and experimentation, moves toward conclusions about relative probability. What is often missed is that the common denominator between initially believing "something" and initially believing "nothing" is "belief." There is no qualitative difference between the two statements, "I don't believe that God exists." And "I believe that God does not exist." Denial of the existence of God is a faith assertion which must then be examined no less rationally than the faith assertion that God does exist. I repeat, to believe that God doesn't exist is no less a faith assertion than the one to believe that God does exist.

Perhaps it is here that the "better alternative" may be found. Is it possible to imagine believing and thinking, not as opposites, but as the expression of a dynamic process of growth and development? I consciously chose the title, "Believing Thinkers and Thinking Believers." This reflects two equally important assumptions on my part. First, anything worth believing can stand up under careful examination. Otherwise there is no way to protect ourselves against believing irrelevant nonsense or deliberate falsehood. Second, believers have an obligation to responsibly make use of their capacity to think carefully. To neglect this responsibility is to end up in a world where authoritarian voices say, "We'll do the thinking, and you do what you're told." When this happens a belief system becomes a prison house of the mind and a tomb for the soul.

Is it not better to embrace and move beyond Augustine's "I believe in order that I may understand," to assert just as sincerely, "I think in order that I may continue to believe"? Surely this balance of "believing thinking" and "thinking believing" is summed up in Jesus' assertion that the greatest commandment is that we "love the Lord (our) God with all (our) heart and with all (our) soul and with all (our) mind" (Mt. 22:37 KJV).

There are those who will protest that there are some things about Christian faith that defy rational explanation. I completely agree. All that I wish to maintain is the important distinction between the "non-rational" and the "irrational." Acknowledgment of the reality of the "non-rational" does not require that one embrace the "irrational." I expect to encounter the "non-rational" in my reflection upon religious reality. A "God" who can be fully understood by my intellect is less than I am, and consequently, is no "God" at all. I do not expect to fully understand. My aim is much more modest. I only seek to grow in understanding. Here I join the company of the Apostle Paul when he confessed, "Brethren, I do not consider that I have made it my own; but one thing I do, forgetting what lies behind and straining forward to what lies ahead, I press on toward the goal for the prize of the heavenly call of God in Christ Jesus" (Phil. 3:13-14 NRSV).

In an essay entitled, "Religious Pluralism and Early Christian Thought," Robert L. Wilken observed that in the earliest centuries of the Christian era "Christians did not make private appeals to faith or claim privileged acess to God; they cheerfully entered the marketplace of ideas" (Robert L. Wilkin, *Remembering the Christian Past* (Grand Rapids, MI: Eerdmans, 1995), p. 38).

Our present era requires the same "cheerful" willingness to engage the "marketplace of ideas." As surely as the early Christian community took on the intellectual scoffers of its day and demonstrated that they could think as rigorously and clearly from a position of belief as others could from a position of unbelief; today's Christian community needs to take up the same challenge. The twenty-first century calls for "believing thinkers" and "thinking believers" for, from the Christian perspective, to decline to do one is to deny the reality of the other. Remember the words of Augustine, "everybody who believes, thinks . . . ."

CHAPTER THREE
Lessons from a Sweetgum Tree that Refused to Die

In mid-winter I made the decision. It was time for the Sweetgum tree in our front yard to go. I had been thinking about it for some time, and had plenty of good reasons to justify the demise of this forty to fifty year old tree. First, the leaves and prickly balls were a mess to clean up and dispose of in the fall. Second, because it was near a power line, the utility people had pruned it into unattractiveness. Third, its gnarled roots protruded from the ground, and frequently bent expensive lawn mower blades. Fourth, I wanted to open up a space where the grandchildren would have more room to play when they came to visit.

Thus, with ample rational justification, from my perspective, I fired up the chainsaw and set to work. I notched the tree on one side and then proceeded to backcut from the other side, the way seasoned firewood cutters always do. As the backcut neared the notch, with my wife watching in anticipation, the tree was supposed to begin a lazy lean from the vertical that would end with the trunk and crown of the Sweetgum tree lying supine in the front yard. From there it would be easy to cut the trunk and limbs into firewood, dispose of the brush, and call it a day.

You know about the "best laid plans of mice and men," don't you? The tree refused to fall. Cut almost completely through, it stood perfectly balanced as though the chainsaw had never touched it. Not to worry. I knew what to do. Having had much experience with cutting trees from my childhood on, I had a sledge hammer and wedges nearby just in case. I quickly lifted the sledge and drove two steel wedges into the backcut in order to shift the weight of the tree and let Isaac Newton and the law of gravity take care of the rest. The tree swayed a bit, balanced itself, and continued its defiant stand.

19

Telling Peggy to stay out of the way, I retrieved a long towing strap from the toolbox on my pickup truck, tossed it across a stout limb, and enlisted my, by now apprehensive, wife to help. Together we threw our combined weight into the strap and pulled with all our might. What happened? Nothing.

Enough time had passed for curious and bemused neighbors to gather. The women clustered around Peggy and talked knowingly of male egos, testosterone, and the tendency of middle-aged men to think they are capable of doing anything, regardless of the potential danger involved. Meanwhile, the guys huddled around me, and we entered into a hurried conspiracy to deliver me from my predicament. Almost miraculously a "come-along" appeared. Eager hands attached one end to the strap I had already thrown around the tree, while more hands tied off the other end of the "come-along" to a large nearby Maple. The ratchet was worked feverishly, and in minutes the deed was done. Human ingenuity, male stubbornness, and the Laws of Physics had combined to bring the Sweetgum tree into crashing submission.

Over the next few days I cut limbs and trunk up into firewood and disposed of the brush. During the remaining weeks of winter I combined the green Sweetgum with my dwindling supply of dry firewood, and Peggy and I enjoyed crackling and popping evening fires in our living room fireplace.

Winter segued into spring, one of the rainiest springs Rutherford County had seen in years. One day in early June I went to check on the progress of four tomato plants Peggy and I had set out a few weeks before. Walking to the plants, I passed two short sections of unsplit tree trunk; all that remained of the old Sweetgum. As I walked past something unusual caught my eye. My mind said, "No, that can't happen." I looked closer and thought, "Well, maybe it can."

One 2 ½ to 3 foot section of the tree trunk lay upon the ground unattached to anything. It was, I thought, dead; dead as could be. Yet, from three separate places the slice of tree trunk was sprouting new limbs and leaves. Remember, I'm not talking about the stump in the front yard with its root system still intact. I'm talking about a 75 – 80 pound section of Sweetgum trunk that I had physically picked up, loaded on a utility trailer, and transported several hundred feet from its original location. As I stared wonderingly at the budding limbs and leaves, it was evident that what was left of the old Sweetgum simply refused to acknowledge that it was dead. Completely detached from its supporting system of roots, it stubbornly clung to life, and valiantly strove to produce new life despite the destructive trauma it had experienced.

Being a reflective sort, the sight of this detached log sprouting new limbs and leaves provided the occasion to sit down and ruminate on the lessons that might be learned. Somehow the circumstances of the tree focused my reflection upon the nature of some interpersonal relationships. My thoughts are offered here as much for my own instruction as for the edification of others.

One thought that came to mind was the human tendency to make purely subjective decisions about things and/or persons; and then develop, in the aftermath, rationally objective reasons to justify the decisions. While, at the beginning of this piece, I listed all the reasons why the tree needed to come down, in retrospect, the truth is that the decision to cut down the old Sweetgum actually preceded any rational reflection upon justifying reasons. Put with brutal bluntness, I cut down the tree because I wanted to cut down the tree. I wanted to, I could, and so I did. It's that simple.

Often we are this way with people as well. They are our neighbors, co-workers, employees, fellow church-members, even family members. We become angry or disappointed or disillusioned or frustrated with them. They have hurt our feelings, injured our pride, have quirky personalities, or they simply get in our way. And so we dispose of them, one way or another, with no more concern than I had for the old Sweetgum tree that cluttered my front yard. We fire them, or get them fired. We exclude them from our circle of friends. We use our influence to get others to cut off contact or social relations with them. In short, we draw a circle that leaves them out.

But it is only after the deed has been done that we formulate systematic, logical reasons for our actions. Such reasons, while focusing on the words and deeds of others, are really intended to justify our own choice to dispose of these people who have become, for one reason or another, troublesome to us. While emphasizing what the cut-off person did that was/is wrong, our reasons really serve to demonstrate how we were/are right.

Such self-justification shields us from having to admit our fears, our prejudices, our weaknesses. After-the-fact reasons keep us from having to say, "I just don't like that person any more." or "How dare she have the temerity to disagree with me?" or "I can't stand the thought that so-and-so is prettier, or smarter, or more likable than I." And so, using the most powerful psychic and social tools at our disposal, we cut them down without the slightest regard for the personal, social, economic, or psychological harm we may do them. They got in our way, so they had to go.

A second thought that occurred to me is how much easier it is to destroy or dispose of another, than it is to learn to value and live with them in spite of their failures and limitations. Most of us aren't very good at maintaining "high maintenance" friends, co-workers, employees, etc. Again, the rationalizations are easy to formulate. "Tom has a bad attitude." "Well, you know, Jane is not from around here." Or "Did you hear what happened to them in that other job, church, civic club, and so forth?" Isn't it fascinating that our own idiosyncratic attributes are the things that make us interesting; while those of another are the qualities that make them weird, undesirable, not able to fit in. Often a person's gifts, abilities, experience, discipline, commitment, integrity, and need are irrelevant. What matters is their personal usefulness to us. As long as they have value for us, we have a place for them in our lives. But, at the point at which they become, or are in danger of becoming, a liability to us, we cut them off and move on to others. And often the sociological phenomenon that we are likely to do things in groups that we would not do by ourselves asserts itself. Thus, with the same ease with which my neighbors aided me in cutting down the no longer wanted Sweetgum tree, others join us in the marginalization of another whose stock has gone down, and who no longer has value for us.

My rumination on the Sweetgum tree that refused to die made me increasingly uncomfortable. For my third thought was that, across the decades, there were persons I had both valued and abandoned in much the same way as I had dealt with the Sweetgum tree. The capacity to perceive the injury others have done to us is remarkable. It is another thing to perceive and acknowledge the injuries we do. Perhaps this is part of what Jesus had in mind when he asked the self-righteous and self-justifying of his day, "Why do you look at the speck of sawdust in your brother's eye, and pay no attention to the plank in your own eye" (Mt.

7:3)? My past is filled with much joy and satisfaction over earlier words and deeds; there are some regrets also. Remember those words from Edward R. Sill's poem, *The Fool's Prayer*, that many of us memorized in high school days:

> *These clumsy feet, still in the mire,*
> *Go crushing blossoms without end;*
> *These hard, well-meaning hands we thrust*
> *Among the heart-strings of a friend.*

Sometimes, no matter how carefully formulated and logical the rationalizations, a look in the mirror of life still causes one to cringe in regret and shame for past actions toward others. We could have been more patient, tried harder, thought longer, valued more highly. But we didn't. And now the other is irretrievably gone. They were "high maintenance" and so we cut them out of our lives, burned them on the brush pile of our failure to evoke more from them than we did, tidied up the mess, and moved on. After all, one can't grieve over the past forever, can one?

Lastly, I thought, "Thank God we don't have the final say about life and worth in the lives of others." I know, the old Sweetgum tree was truly doomed. Days later that rainy, wet June transmuted into a hot and dry July. Under the blistering sun of mid-summer, the moisture remaining in the log evaporated. The tender, new leaves withered, cracks appeared in the trunk, and by August all signs of life were gone. I had, in fact, killed the Sweetgum tree.

But trees are not human beings, and thus two things remain true. One, the fact that I may have declared the death of another person by cutting them off, abandoning them, withdrawing my friendship from them, or dismissing them from my presence does not mean that they have no subsequent value. In fact, some have done quite well, and have accomplished much without the "blessing" of my involvement in their lives. They didn't need me and my approval nearly as much as I needed to think they did. Consign them to oblivion as I may have done, they refused to wither, dry-up, and die. Why? Because their value as persons lay within them, not in the value, or lack thereof, I wished to assign.

The second truth is that I also have, from time to time, been cut off, abandoned, dismissed, experienced revoked friendship, and been ignored. It's hard. It hurts. The scars are ugly. The trauma is profound. Nevertheless, I still live as well. For my life, my vitality, my usefulness, my value does not lie in the estimate, or lack thereof, that others assign to me. Human beings, by God's grace, live not from the outside-in, but from the inside-out.

Each of us is God's creation, God's creature. God is the One who has caused us to be, and God is the One who sustains our being. Life is more than our reputation, more than our economic security, more than the esteem of others, more even than breath within a body. And so, while others may sully reputation, jeopardize economic security, withdraw esteem, and even physically kill; others cannot destroy our lives. Others did not cause our life to be, and others cannot declare its non-being. Both I and you have life and value, whether these qualities are assigned by others or not. We have life and value because the God who created us says we have life and value. And so, by God's grace, we refuse to be consigned to the brush heap of oblivion, no matter what others have done or circumstances have wrought. We do so simply by continuing to live, and by striving to lead productive lives.

And so, here is the end of the thing. Will I cut down trees in the future? Probably. Will I, from time to time, continue to injure those with whom I share life? Almost certainly. But my fervent prayer is that my experience with the Sweetgum tree will cause me to think more carefully beforehand, so that I have need to do less rationalizing self-justification in the aftermath. Why? Because there is neither an inexhaustible supply of trees, nor is there an infinite number of relationships I can get by without.

CHAPTER FOUR
God in the Hands of an Angry Sinner

Though not qualifying as the "Winter of My Discontent," I must admit that it was the "Spring of My Acute Distress." In rapid fire succession a dear friend died after a long but losing battle with colon cancer. My wife fell backward across our kitchen dishwasher door and shattered a wrist beyond full recovery. A second valued friend collapsed suddenly in the midst of a Sunday morning worship service and died moments later of massive heart failure. Shortly over a week later cardiac bypass surgery on a third friend went badly awry and she was left brain dead. I stood with her husband and children as the medical professionals disconnected all the apparatus that kept her respiratory system functioning. Our second and last child left home to explore and make a place for himself in the world, leaving Peggy and me with, if you don't count the dog and the cats, an empty nest.

All these events were set within the context of a two year period that called upon me to care for a mother left paralyzed and speechless by a stroke, and impoverished by a political/economic system that seems more concerned about the bottom line profits of insurance companies and the health care industry, than about the quality of life of the aging and infirm. Those two years also led me to the threshold of age fifty, when, as a young man, I thought I would be just hitting my stride as minister, academician, preacher, and teacher. Instead, the threshold of fifty found me unemployed and forced to liquidate investments laid back for future retirement in order to repair a worn out septic system and replace a leaking roof.

As an undergraduate student in the late 1960's I was introduced to Jonathan Edwards' famous sermon, "Sinners in the Hands of An Angry

God" in a Survey of American Literature course. Subsequent academic and professional study have caused me to read Edwards on more than one occasion since then. While not always agreeing with him, I must concur with others that Jonathan Edwards was the first indigenous American Christian theologian. But my purpose is not to explore and critique the content of Edwards' "Sinners in the Hands of An Angry God." Rather, I am bent upon exploring the implications of "God in the Hands of An Angry Sinner."

While my personal reflections may have something of the self-pitying tone of a modern Jeremiad, they are not intended to be. I am astute enough to recognize that I am not the only person ever called upon to deal with difficult circumstances, nor were my circumstances the worst imaginable. I certainly do not wish to imply that my grief over the loss of dear friends was more profound than that suffered by their spouses, children, and parents. I am acutely aware that I am not the only person charged with caring for an aging parent, or who has struggled with difficult economic circumstances. Rather, on my own behalf and on the behalf of others in similar circumstances, I am attempting to explore the reality that, deep down, I have been angry about these things, and I am convinced that this anger is not entirely inappropriate.

Over the centuries Christians have been taught to repress and deny the legitimate human emotion of anger. With biblical prooftexts such as, ". . . let not the sun go down on your wrath" (Eph. 4:26 KJV) and ". . . whosoever is angry with his brother . . . shall be in danger of judgment . . ." (Mt. 5:22 KJV), we have built a theology that suggests that anger is essentially sinful and that there is no place for wrath in the life of the Christian believer. To do so is to ignore the ". . . without a cause . . ." in the words of Jesus and the "be ye angry, and sin not . . ." in the counsel of the Apostle Paul. A careful reading of the biblical record will reveal that legitimate anger, as such, is never deplored. Rather, we are called upon to discipline and channel the anger properly, so that it does not become destructive to ourselves and others (Ps. 37:8; Pr. 14:7, 16:32, 19:11; Ec. 7:9; Mt. 5:22; Ja. 1:19).

There are circumstances in our world, in both the macrocosm and the microcosm, that are deserving of legitimate indignation. In the larger setting it is necessary to note only the wanton destruction of life occasioned by humankind's seeming determination, in recent decades, to step backward into tribalism. The horrors of terrorism and ethnic cleansing, and the futile attempts being made to impede this spiral of atrocity, should evoke anger on a broad scale, regardless of one's religious identity, political persuasion, economic status, or genetic background. At the microcosmic level of the individual, the grief and sense of loss occasioned by the death of a loved one, the ravages of a terminal illness, the loss of a job, the rupture of a relationship, or the betrayal of a friend carries its own measure of anger.

To deny and repress legitimate anger often leads to depression, or erupts in violence that is destructive to self and others. In the name of physical, mental, emotional, and spiritual good health, anger is not to be denied, but acknowledged and dealt with appropriately. Anger is not the opposite of love; love's opposite is indifference. To be angry is not to deny love. On the contrary, anger is one of the ways love expresses itself, for anger is one of the human emotions that says we care, what happens makes a difference, and that we are alive.

What is perhaps most difficult to own is the reality that sometimes we are even angry with God. Again, here we are often the victims of bad theology emerging from poor biblical interpretation. We have been told from infancy, "Anger is bad, and God's going to get you if you're bad. So never admit anger, especially anger with God."

The truth is that I'm not sure that God is not more pleased with the honest expression of anger on our part than He is with the supine piety devoid of passion that is often passed off as Christian spirituality. One has only to read the Bible to discover the anger toward God expressed by such notable personalities as Sarah, Moses, Job, Jeremiah, the Psalmist, and others. God didn't "ZAP" them because of their passionate expressions of disappointment and pain. On the contrary, it was out of the crucible of their anger that God forged and refined their personalities. Praise God for Sarah's mocking laughter, Moses' blow to the rock, Job's refusal to feign guilt, and Jeremiah's insistence that he had an opinion too. Yes, they knew the rebuke of God, but in each instance, it was their lack of faith or refusal to be obedient that was rebuked, not their legitimate anger.

How then do we deal with the reality that sometimes we are angry with God? This "angry sinner" has a few suggestions to offer. First, spend some time hugging and kissing your babies and grandbabies. And if you don't have any of your own, go and find someone who will let you hug and kiss theirs. For such a tangible expression of love reminds us that, no matter what the circumstances, our descendants, those who, by our own volition we have caused to be, are never far from our thoughts and hearts. Thus it is with God, our Creator, the One who has caused us to be and Who sustains our being. We are always enveloped in the loving mind and heart of God. And as surely as much human anger toward one another is assuaged by a tender caress and a loving kiss; our anger at God will melt away in the cruciform embrace and the "Father forgive them . . ." kiss. It is here that we discover things are made right, not so much by restitution as by reconciliation, and our demands for justice are transmuted into tears of gratitude because we have found mercy.

Second, remember that God gets angry too. I'm not talking about peevish petulance, but about genuine, towering, righteous indignation over the recalcitrant selfishness and self-destructive *hubris* (pride) of fallen humanity living in a fallen world. Consultation with a good biblical concordance will reveal dozens of places where the biblical writers refer to the anger, wrath, indignation, etc. of God. Thus, it is not inappropriate to conclude that human anger is one of the evidences that we are created in the image and likeness of God. Classical Christian theology affirms the omnipotence (supreme power), omniscience (universal knowledge), and creativity of God. While these divine attributes say something about God, they say something about human beings as well. Truly, I am not all powerful, but I do have some power. Certainly I am not all knowing, but I do know some things. Obviously, I cannot cause to be *ex nihilo* (out of nothing), but I do have creative gifts. If it is true that my limited power, knowledge, and creativity, when rightly used, reflect the qualities of God, then it is also true that my anger, rightly focused and expressed, also reflects the quality of God.

Third, remember that in the person and work, in the life, ministry, and atoning death of Jesus Christ, God elected to absorb the totality of human sinfulness into the Divine Self and cut short its ultimate destructive power. Thus God says, "Give your anger to me. I can handle it. If you insist upon wallowing in it, or upon pouring it out indiscriminately on those around you, the anger will ultimately destroy you. Give it to Me and I will teach you to use the energy engendered by anger in constructive, redemptive ways."

Finally, remember that while anger may be a place to be for a time, it is no place to live indefinitely. Anger expresses itself along the progressive continuum of human emotion. It is preceded by disappointment, shock, loss, pain, and grief. It is followed by catharsis, adjustment, resolution, and reintegration into the ongoing processes of life. The house of anger is not a dwelling place, it is simply a station along the way. While we must stop there for a time, we must also move on.

Most often anger is the by-product of grief. Someone or something has died. It may have been a person who played a significant role in our understanding of ourselves. It may have been a hope, or dream, or aspiration. It may have been a friendship, a career, or a marriage. But now they, or it, are dead. We have been reminded of the fragile mortality of others, ourselves, and of the ideas we hold dear. A vacuum has been created in our existence that needs to be filled. And for a time the vacuum is filled by anger engendered by disappointment and loss, for we feel that those whom we held dear, or that which we valued highly, have been swallowed up in death.

It is here that the biblical message of God's redemptive purpose in Jesus Christ must be listened to carefully. For the biblical message declares that fragile human mortality is not swallowed up in death. On the contrary, Paul says our "mortality [is] swallowed up in life" (II Cor. 5:4 KJV). Grief and loss, and their accompanying anger, do not have the final word in the life of the person of authentic Christian faith. For the Christian believer, both the last and ultimate word belongs to God "for we walk by faith, not by sight . . ." (II Cor. 5:7 KJV).

CHAPTER FIVE
Knowing God is More Than a Warm Fuzzy Feeling

D o you sometimes wake up in the morning with a dull ache in your forehead and the sense that someone is tightening a tourniquet around your head? On these days, does the inside of your mouth feel like you think it would if a herd of elephants had walked through the night before? Do you have the impression that rather than sleeping, you've just been unconscious for the last several hours? And now life has to be faced. The shower must be taken, the kids must be fed and gotten off to school, and the drive to the plant, or the office, or the store must be made.

As a confessing Christian I must admit that when these occasional days come along, I don't feel very "saved." I don't feel enfolded in the arms of God's love. I don't feel, to borrow a line, that "God's in his heaven, and all's right with the world." And it is on days like this that I'm profoundly grateful my relationship to God is not founded upon how I "feel" but upon what God has done, and continues to do, in and through the person and work of Jesus Christ.

One of the troubling things about the packaging of contemporary Christianity is its emphasis upon "feeling" as the primary indicator of an intimate personal relationship with God. Many preachers seem to suggest that knowing and being known by God is primarily an emotional experience. The result is that religious experience is reduced to a subjective feeling of well-being. To know God is to feel warm and accepted, safe and secure, happy and content. Knowing God is a "warm fuzzy feeling."

By now I suspect many of you are wondering, "What's wrong with that?" I'm glad you asked. The answer is, "several things." At the outset, such an approach is excessively subjective and essentially self-centered. By placing paramount importance upon individual feeling, the

30

measure of the reality of God's activity in the world is dependent upon the emotional content of the individual's sense of well-being. Thus, no matter how eloquently, or loudly, we talk about divine sovereignty, biblical authority, etc., the individual makes himself or herself the ultimate measure of the reality of divine truth. It is from God if it makes me feel good, and if it doesn't make me feel good, it is not from God.

This excessive emphasis upon the "feeling" content of religious experience also tends to encourage childlike dependence, rather than fostering a growing Christian maturity. Here the problem is our tendency to confuse "dependence" with "faith." While they are akin to one another, they are not synonymous, and we get into trouble when we seek to use the terms interchangeably. Certainly Jesus placed great emphasis upon the childlike faith that should be found in the lives of those wishing to enter the kingdom of heaven (Mt. 18:1 – 4). But a careful reading of the text will reveal that the chief quality of that childlike faith is "humility," not neurotic dependence. It is also worthwhile to note it was in the context of Paul's rebuke of the neurotic self-centeredness of the Corinthian believers that he said, "When I was a child, I spoke as a child, I understood as a child, I thought as a child: but when I became a man [a mature person], I put away childish things" (I Cor. 13:11 KJV).

A third problem posed by an excessive focus upon the feeling of well-being associated with experiencing God is that it tends to neglect the challenges to complacency, pride, and abuse of power that are also associated with being confronted by God. It glosses over issues of sin, repentance, and the need to face the consequences of our actions. It knows little of Isaiah's "woe is me, for I am undone" (Is. 6:5), or of Jeremiah's "burning fire shut up in my bones" (Jer. 20:9). Tending to focus upon the emotional content of Luke's story of the loving father's warm embrace of the returning Prodigal Son, it fails to recall that this moving event was preceded by the fact that the son "came to himself [to his senses]" (Lk. 15:17) and said, "Father, I have sinned . . ." (Lk. 15:18, 21).

The problem lies in the desire to experience God only as indulgent, warm, loving parent; never as righteous judge. The truth is that sometimes my relationship with God does not make me feel "warm" and "fuzzy." Rather, face to face with the radical holiness of God, I feel caught, confronted, guilty, judged, rebuked, and called upon to repent. And that is as it should be, because sometimes I need to be caught, confronted, found guilty, judged, rebuked, and called to repentance. Many contemporary Christians are awash in a sentimental sea of what Dietrich Bonhoeffer called "cheap grace." The consequence of such shallow emotionalism has been the loss of a sense of awe in the presence of the Divine, and a corresponding deterioration of a sense of personal accountability for our actions. Stripped of transcendent "otherness," God has been reduced to the indulgent grandparent who will give us whatever we ask for, and is always willing to play "snuggle bunny" with us.

Finally, an excessive emphasis upon the warm emotional content of a relationship with God often leaves the perplexed believer, who is struggling with the complex realities of life, with the sense that these struggles are the consequence of some personal spiritual problem or failure. While this may be true some of the time, it is not necessarily true all of the time.

An overemphasis upon the "warm fuzziness" of knowing God can create the impression that "If I'm not on top of the world all of the time, something is spiritually wrong with me." While external circumstances and inward spiritual condition may have a relationship to one another, they do not automatically stand in one-to-one correspondence. To use one of the quaint expressions of my mother's rural Alabama upbringing, "we can have the world by the tail in a downhill pull" (i.e., everything around us can be going about as well as it can possibly go) and we can still be as carnal and self-centered as it is possible for us to be. On the other hand, it is also possible for us to be suffering under the crushing burdens of life gone awry, while living in a profoundly intimate and meaningful relationship to God. Much that happens to us is the direct consequence of our own personal sin and self-centeredness, but everything that happens to us is not our fault. Sometimes we suffer the consequences of the sins of others. And sometimes we are caught in the throes of circumstances (i.e., disease, natural disaster, accident) that seem to have no discernable cause. Such circumstances may leave us distraught, depressed, and at the limit of our resources. But the fact that something is wrong in our world does not automatically mean there is something wrong between us and God.

Once these cautions have been taken into consideration, the question still remains, "How does one attempt to assess the reality and quality of one's relationship to God?" I would begin by suggesting that it is important, first and foremost, to remember that, from the Christian perspective, such a relationship is God initiated. By this I mean that any meaningful relation with the Divine is predicated upon the reality that God has chosen to disclose God's Self in the midst of human experience. In many ways the profound insight of Augustine of Hippo's *Confessions* may be summarized in the statement, "God, I searched for You, and I searched for You, and I searched for You; and You found me!" All exclusively human attempts to give shape and content to an experience with God end in "babel," (Gen. 11) because they ignore the truth that the relationship is primarily Divine/Human, and only secondarily Human/Divine. Thus we must recall that, while not denying that the relationship is a double-search, the focus of knowing and being known by God is *theocentric* (God centered), not *anthropocentric* (human centered).

Second, we must maintain the understanding that our experience with God is a multifaceted relationship. This is one reason why the appropriate use of the "parent" metaphor is helpful in understanding how we experience God. As surely as, in a healthy parent/child relationship, the child experiences the loving parent as provider, nurturer, and protector, she/he also experiences the parent as teacher, disciplinarian, and judge. In such a relationship, the same caring parent who enfolds in the warm and loving arms of acceptance also confronts and holds accountable. The point is that knowing God is not devoid of warm, fuzzy feelings; but that it is not confined to such emotional content.

When we remain focused upon the multifaceted nature of the Divine/Human relationship, we are better able to appreciate the diversity of Christian experience, and are less likely to measure the spirituality of others by our own. From time to time we encounter another whose experience with God has more or less emotional content than our own, or evidences more or less evangelistic zeal than ours, or is shaped by more or less intellectual reflection than ours. If we make our own experience the lens through which the validity and authenticity of everyone else's is measured, we often become harshly judgmental and condemnatory. The fact that someone else's experience with God is different from ours does not necessarily mean that they, or we, are at the wrong place. It may only mean we are at different places.

Third, from the human side, knowing and being known by God is a dynamic, growing, maturing relationship. One thing this means is that at different places in our pilgrimage, different aspects of this multifaceted relationship may increase or decrease in place and value. Most husbands and wives will confess that, as newly weds in their twenties, early stages of the marriage relationship were primarily focused upon sexual attraction and gratification. There is nothing inherently wrong here. But it is also true that for those who built a vital and enduring relationship, while such libidinal drives did not cease to be important, both learned to value and celebrate other aspects of their own and their mate's personhood as well.

Often the Christian doctrine of salvation is spoken of in terms of regeneration, sanctification, and glorification. The initial transforming awareness of God is regeneration, a new birth. Ultimately and finally, we shall "know as we are known," (I Cor. 13:12) and be, in and through Jesus Christ, as He is (I Jn. 3:2). This is glorification. Meanwhile, the process of growing and maturing into the person God has always intended that we be is sanctification. It is here that we as Christian believers "live and move and have our being" (Acts 17:28 KJV). Between the "already" and the "not yet" of God's redemptive purpose in Jesus Christ, it is appropriate for us to say both, "We have been saved." and "We are being saved." In this unfolding process of transformation, we should learn to value every aspect of God's disclosure of Divine personhood to us. For, as surely as it is true of loving parent/child and spousal relationships, God is always more "for us" and "to us" than we are able to discern through the lens of our own personal subjectivity.

Lastly, it is important to remember that the Christian believer's relationship to God is filled with hope and anticipation. Paul could write, "For now we see through a glass, darkly; but then face to face: now I know in part; but then shall I know even as also I am known" (I Cor. 13:12 KJV). To judge the reality of relationship to God exclusively on the basis of present emotional content, personal suffering, intellectual insight, or any other aspect is to forget that the experiences of "this present time are not worthy to be compared with the glory which shall be revealed ..." (Rom. 8:18 KJV).

Without doubt, the emotional feeling of acceptance and security (sometimes expressed as "warm fuzzy feelings") is an aspect of the believing Christian's experience. While it would be wrong to deny this reality, it is equally mistaken to present the Christian hope in a form that suggests that "warm fuzzy feelings" are the sum total of an authentic experience with God. Knowing God is More Than a Warm Fuzzy Feeling.

CHAPTER SIX
There's Nobody Left But You and Me, and I'm Not So Sure of You Anymore

One can hardly turn on the TV news or pick up a daily paper anymore without seeing some reference to the phenomenon of "fundamentalism" in the modern world. The word "fundamentalist" has become another of those words we lob, like an artillery shell, at persons whom we do not understand, or with whom we disagree. Unfortunately, while the use of the word "fundamentalism" is ubiquitous in our society, many have little or no understanding of the concept itself.

The truth is that fundamentalists come in all shapes and sizes. They are liberal, conservative, and moderate. They are male and female. They are heterosexual and homosexual. They are religiously orthodox and heretical. They are Christian, Islamic, and atheistic. They are pro-life and pro-abortion. They are proponents of radical anti-firearms legislation, and they are members of the NRA. Fundamentalism knows no racial, ethnic, cultural, political, religious, or gender constraints. While most often the term is associated with extreme religious conservatism, I maintain that "fundamentalism is a mindset—not a theological position."

One of the distinguishing characteristics of the twentieth century was a sharp rise in fundamentalist ideologies. While most tend to think in terms of Jerry Falwell's Moral Majority, or single-issue crusades that appear in all religious denominations, these are only religio-cultural instances of a much wider phenomenon. Whether one explores the emergence of survivalist groups and underground militias, the movements of major political parties to purify their ranks, or the many calls for economic, educational, and social reform, one finds the fundamentalist phenomenon manifesting itself throughout the world's cultures.

Often periods of time are identified by a primary phenomenon that gives shape to the era. Thus we often refer to the eighteenth century as "The Age of Reason," or the period from 1920 – 1950 as "The Totalitarian Era." In this vein it may be said that since 1970 the world in general, and American culture in particular, has experienced the "Era of Fundamentalism."

Given this broad-ranging diversity, how does one go about identifying a fundamentalist? Too often we look in the wrong place. We tend to examine core beliefs and values. This causes us to focus upon those who hold highly conservative or traditionalist points of view. The end result is that we identify only the "fundamentalism of the right" and fail to recognize the fundamentalisms of the "left" or the "center." Our mistake is that we associate fundamentalism with the core beliefs and values of persons rather than in their mindset. Thus we need to explore the identifying characteristics of the fundamentalist mindset, regardless of the particular flavor of the fundamentalism we are examining.

The fundamentalist personality is one who is threatened by any challenge to his or her world-view. Various factors have led to the selection of a particular lens through which all reality is filtered. It matters little what the content of the underlying presupposition happens to be. It may be that "capitalism is the only viable economic system"; or that "America is destined by God to be the most powerful nation in the world"; or that "the Constitution guarantees every citizen the right to possess an assault weapon." The fundamentalist senses that whenever her or his world-view is questioned at any point, the one doing the questioning is seeking to undermine the order of the world as it should be.

This first characteristic leads logically to a second. The fundamentalist personality tends to demonize anyone who appears to disagree with her or his position. The adversary is painted in broad, bold strokes as the most insidious creature imaginable. One has only to look at the rhetoric of politics to see this demonization of the adversary at work. The fundamentalist's need to claim the moral, or theological, or political, or social "high ground" leads to the caricature of the other as the polar opposite of all that is good and right and true. Those today who decry the "politics of personal destruction" have first-hand experience of this fundamentalist tendency to demonize the adversary.

A third identifying characteristic of the fundamentalist mindset is its tendency to focus upon a few major points that are seen as free-standing truths beyond examination or challenge. On behalf of fundamentalists, regardless of flavor, it must be said that they can simply and clearly articulate their views. The fundamentalist assumes that his or her basic conclusions about reality are axiomatic. The sheer assertion of them demonstrates their validity. And all "right-thinking" persons will recognize their inherent truth.

The fundamentalist recognizes that all do not subscribe to his position, a fourth characteristic. This reality is dealt with by dismissing those holding an alternative viewpoint as dishonest, deluded, dumb, or deceived. To not hold the fundamentalist's viewpoint is to be lacking in integrity or intelligence or both. Surely any honest and right-thinking person sees things as the fundamentalist does.

The tendency to demonize those who disagree, and to question the integrity of their personhood, leads to a fifth characteristic of the fundamentalist mindset. The loyalty or orthodoxy of others is always interpreted in personal terms. The fundamentalist is the archetypal "true-believer" and everyone wishing to associate with him/her must be a "true-believer" as well. Fundamentalists essentially say, "If you love me, you will agree with me." They tend to hear phrases such as "I don't agree with you" or "I don't think your conclusion is correct" as assertions of "I don't like you" or "I don't trust you." Fundamentalists, because they are essentially insecure persons, need continual reassurance that others hold them in high esteem. Consequently they often assume the posture of "there's nobody left but you and me; and I'm not so sure of you anymore."

This leads logically to a sixth, and possibly the most disturbing, characteristic of the fundamentalist mindset. If a fundamentalist feels forced to make a choice between conceding some point or sacrificing some person, it is the person who is sacrificed. The need always to be right forces the fundamentalist to adopt a "my way or the highway" approach toward others. To use another analogy, the fundamentalist is perfectly willing to allow a person to ride his train. But the person must remember that it is the fundamentalist's train. And it goes where the fundamentalist wants it to go. And if you don't want to get hurt, you don't forget, not even for a moment, whose train you are riding.

Once one understands that fundamentalism is a mindset, one learns to pay less attention to ideology and more to personality. Among the fundamentalists I have known were the president of a theologically moderate denominational college, a small town brick mason, a highly placed executive in a major international corporation, the director of a church choir, the manager of a small business, and a town drunk. These women and men illustrate a wide range of social, economic, cultural, religious, and ethnic diversity. Yet they were, and are, all fundamentalists. They are fundamentalists not because of what they subscribe to as core values and beliefs, but because of the manner in which they maintain their personal point of view against all alternative ways of perceiving and understanding. They are fundamentalists, not because of *what* they think, but because of *how* they think and *how* they relate to others who think differently.

The noted seventeenth-century philosopher and essayist, John Locke, wrote his *Essay Concerning Human Understanding*, his *Two Treatises on Government*, and his *A Letter Concerning Toleration* in response to the *absolutisms*, another word for "fundamentalisms," of his day. Locke saw the fundamentalist mindset asserting itself in three primary expressions: epistemological (the science of knowledge) absolutism, political absolutism, and religious absolutism. In the first work Locke protested against the claims of certainty of knowledge in his day. His conviction regarding the role of personal experience in our interpretation of knowledge caused him to counsel caution toward all who claimed to have absolute handles on the truth. While there may be absolute, free-standing truth, human subjectivity knows only "truth as I (we) see it." Fundamentalists of all flavors tend to forget their own subjectivity.

In the *Two Treatises on Government* Locke called for the abandonment of government by divine-right monarchy in favor of a consensual social contract through which the ruler ruled with the consent of the governed. The tendency of fundamentalism to ally itself with rigidly hierarchical decision-making needs to hear Locke's assertion that the role of any governing structure (religious, political, educational, and so forth) is that of serving the needs of its constituency, not that of exerting manipulative control over the governed.

In *A Letter Concerning Toleration*, Locke argued that no religious group is justified in forcing its beliefs upon others. No religious personality (minister, priest, ayatollah, or layperson) is justified in claiming to be so certain of the Divine will that he/she is justified in resorting to psychological intimidation, social coercion, and/or physical force to impose her/his understanding on others. This is a good caution for those today who espouse religious absolutism and intolerance; or who tend to present their political, social, or ethical agendas as religious articles of faith.

Violent expressions of the fundamentalist mentality are epidemic in modern culture along a continuuium that includes religious, social, and political stances from the right, the left, and the middle. Sometimes the violence expresses itself in car bombs and terrorist atrocities; sometimes in shrill screams that consign anyone who holds a different viewpoint to the fires of hell; sometimes in deliberate efforts to destroy the credibility, career, and reputation of another. Quite often such fundamentalist stances are asserted on the authority of Divine Revelation: "the Bible says," or "Allah commands it," or "God revealed it to me and told me to tell you."

The Apostle Paul told the Philippian Christians: *Let this mind be in you, which was also in Christ Jesus: Who, being in the form of God, thought it not robbery to be equal with God: But made himself of no reputation, and took upon him the form of a servant, and was made in the likeness of men: And being found in fashion as a man he humbled himself, and became obedient unto death, even the death of the cross. (Philippians 2:5 – 8).*

When I run across someone who asserts that they know the mind of God with absolute certitude, I test their truth-claim against what Paul describes as the characteristics of the "mind of Christ": Lack of concern for personal reputation; a servant attitude; the willingness to identify with the circumstances of others; gracious humility; and a genuine concern to relate redemptively toward others, even at great personal sacrifice. If I find these qualities I am inclined to listen carefully and respectfully to what they have to say. If, on the other hand, what I find is excessive egoism, an overbearing attitude, detachment and lack of empathy for the circumstances of others, excessive pride, and harsh judgmentalism; I find it difficult to patiently hear what they have to say. For some strange reason, I think those who claim to speak on God's behalf should reflect, in their lives and conduct, the qualities of the God on whose behalf they claim to speak.

(Much of the content of this essay was published previously under the title "Fundamentalism is a Mindset – Not a Theological Position" in *Mature Years*, a publication of the United Methodist Church, Summer, 2000.)

CHAPTER SEVEN
Heads, Hearts, and Hormones –
Good Religion Needs Them All

The complex nature of the human creature is one of the marvels of God's creative activity. To be a human being is to be a dynamic inter-relationship of rational reflection, emotional feeling, and primal hormonal drives. More so than in any other creature, these three clusters of realities express themselves in every aspect of our being. We are thinking beings. We are feeling beings. And we are beings driven by bio-chemical interactions beyond the scope of our rational reflection or emotional need.

Nowhere is this reality more manifest than in the realm of human religious experience. The Divine/Human – Human/Divine encounter is one of heads, hearts, and hormones; and good religion needs them all. For it is in the dynamic inter-relationship of rational cognition, creaturely feeling, and primal drive that human beings encounter and respond to God's revelation of God's self to humankind.

Certainly since the 17th century, in the aftermath of Descartes famous dictum, *Cogito Ergo Sum* (I Think Therefore I Am), much attention has been focused upon the rational dimensions of human personhood. Human beings think. Yes, it is true that other animals think as well. They learn. They solve problems. But the evidence available to date seems to indicate that only human beings think reflectively, i.e., only human beings think about thinking. My wife's Yorkshire Terrier, Clancy, may very well think, "I am hungry, or cold, or frightened." But only human beings ask, "*Why* do I *think* I am hungry, or cold, or afraid?"

One of the reasons philosophical idealism has historically been such an influential vehicle for Christian theological reflection is its foundational assumption that Ultimate Reality is more like Spirit or Mind than like matter or stuff. Philosophical idealism assumes there is an underlying rationality in all existence. And, when this assumption is passed through the matrix of the Judaeo-Christian religious tradition, it is asserted that human rationality reflects Divine rationality. To be rational is an aspect of what it means to be created in the image and likeness of God. To know God's will is to think God's thoughts after Him. The Bible expresses this rational aspect of humankind's relationship with the Creator in its emphasis upon wisdom (OT – *hokma*, NT – *sophia*) and word (OT – *dabar*, NT – *logos*).

Paralleling this focus upon the rational dimension of human religious experience, especially since the post-Reformation, there has been an equally focused emphasis upon the "feeling" content inherent in the Divine/Human encounter. F.D.E. Schleiermacher protested excessive preoccupation with the rational in his classic *On Religion: Speeches to Its Cultured Despisers*. Under the influence of Pietism, Schleiermacher traced human religious experience to the creaturely feeling of absolute dependence in the Divine presence. In a similar, but not identical fashion, Rudolf Otto, in his *The Idea of the Holy*, spoke of humankind's encounter with the *mysterium tremendum et fascinans* and the feelings of "awe" and "dread" evoked by such an encounter. In the 20th century this emphasis upon the "feeling" content of religious experience was expressed, in its most rational form, in the thought of Paul Tillich, and in its most non-rational form in the syrupy sentimentalism of much popular religion still shaped by the emotionalism of the Second Great Awakening. Such emotionalism tends to collapse a relationship with God into the experience of "warm fuzzy" feelings.

While subject to abuse, this emphasis upon the emotional content of human religious experience is deeply rooted in the biblical revelation. One has only to follow the somber strains of grief, or the lyrical notes of joy one finds in the Psalmist; or to hear the message of abiding love in Hosea, to note this truth. In the New Testament, Paul's affirmation of, while cautioning against the dangers in, ecstatic spirituality serve to draw attention to the deep and profound emotional content of the Apostle's own relationship to God.

Ludwig Feuerbach, in his two works, *The Essence of Religion* and *The Essence of Christianity*, rocked the foundations of traditional religious belief by suggesting that, rather than being creatures created in the image and likeness of God, we human beings have, in fact, created God in our own image as the by-product of our instinctive interaction with the circumstances of our existence. This view asserts that God is no more than our best conception of ourselves projected upon the backdrop of our experience.

Standing on the shoulders of Feuerbach, such influential thinkers as Sigmund Freud, the father of modern psychoanalysis, and B.F. Skinner, the father of behavioristic psychology, have effectively reduced the understanding of human behavior to no more or less than the sum of our hormonal needs and instinctive drives. In *The Future of an Illusion* Freud argued that religion functions as a coping mechanism that assists in dealing with the accumulated guilt and resentment of our childhood. In *Beyond Freedom and Dignity* Skinner asserts that all our actions are explainable on the assumption that we are entirely determined creatures whose actions are the consequences of the physiological mechanisms we have developed, through the processes of random natural selection and the survival of the fittest, in order to cope with our environment's threats to our existence.

While one's first reaction is one of repudiation of such assertions, honesty compels the acknowledgment that this naturalistic emphasis is not wholly without warrant in the biblical literature. The creation narrative's emphasis upon the creaturely identity of human beings with other animals, and our nature as red dirt (*adam*) enlivened by the "breath of God" (Gen. 2:7), serve to remind us that, in spite of our pretentiousness, that which physically separates us from other primates, at the level of DNA, is quite minute.

One of my favorite childhood cartoon characters often sang, "I am what I am and that's all that I am. I'm Popeye the Sailor Man." As human beings we are what we are. As stated earlier, to be a human being is to be a dynamic inter-relationship of rational reflection (we think and choose), emotional feeling (we sense and respond), and primal instinctive hormonal drives (we are compelled and driven). For the believing Christian, this truth is not an occasion for despair, but is, in fact, a truth to be embraced and celebrated. For knowledge of God is profoundly rooted in our minds, our hearts, and in our hormones. Our aim should not be to deny any of these realities, but to relate them properly to one another.

    If I am correct in what I have asserted thus far, and I am certainly aware there are those who will dispute with me, the question that remains to be answered is, "How do we, as persons of faith, fully acknowledge the complexity of human personhood and the importance of the contributions of heads, hearts, and hormones to our experience of God?" Several principles suggest themselves for consideration: The first I would call the Principle of Correlation. By this I mean each aspect of human personhood must be maintained in proper relationship to the others. While I am a thinking being, I am not just a highly sophisticated biological computer. While I am profoundly moved by emotion, I am more than a tangle of sentiments and emotional needs. This is evidenced by the use of my rational capacities to control and manage my emotional responses. And, without doubt, I am a creature compelled by the primal instinctive drives to survive, reproduce, satisfy hunger, and sleep in safety. Our task, particularly as rational beings, is to correlate these realities in such a way that they are appropriately balanced.

    A second principle may be called the *Shema*/Augustine Principle. When asked the greatest of the commandments, Jesus reminded his questioner of Israel's ancient confession, "Hear O Israel, the Lord our God is One Lord. And you shall love the Lord your God with all your heart, and with all your soul, and with all your might [mind]" (Deut. 6:4-5; Mat. 22:37). When asked for a principle to guide moral/ethical decision making, Augustine of Hippo replied, "Love God, and do what you will." Love of God and godly love are the keys to all human emotional responses. When *agapeistic* love is given pre-eminence, our emotions are refined by rational reflection and prevented from descending into undisciplined passion or sentimental self-indulgence.

    A third principle I call the *Sine Sera* Principle. The English word *sincere* is based upon the Latin phrase *sine sera*, which literally means to be "without wax." The phrase refers to the unscrupulous practice of many ancient sculptors who filled flaws in their work with polished bee's wax. The *Sine Sera* Principle is then a principle of integrity, of wholeness, of authenticity. The dynamic inter-relationship of cognitive, emotive, and instinctive personhood may be separated only for the purpose of discussion. The *Sine Sera* Principle insists that we recognize that the human creature is a "psychosomatic" (psycho-physical) whole, the diverse aspects of whose personhood are so integrally related that it is not possible

44

to speak of one without appropriate acknowledgment of the others.

Finally, I suggest the usefulness of the Tevye Principle. Those who love the musical, *Fiddler on the Roof*, appreciate the endearing character of Tevye, who, caught in a world of contradictions, attempts to make sense of it all. In one scene one of the villagers makes a categorical assertion and Tevye says, "You're right." A second villager asserts just the opposite and Tevye says, "You're right." A third villager, puzzled by his response says to Tevye, "How can they both be right? They said opposite things." And Tevye agrees, "You're right."

The Tevye Principle cautions against the danger of uncritical reductionistic thinking. Excessive emphasis upon a single aspect of human personhood often leads to contradiction as that one aspect is elevated to the level of a single, free standing truth which is then used as a standard by which one measures all other truth. To see humankind as only rational, or only emotional, or only instinctive is to forget that truth is a multi-faceted jewel whose sublime beauty can be appreciated only when viewed as a unity, not as isolated facets. And examine as carefully as one may, the mysteries of the jewel are still never fully revealed.

Heads, hearts, and hormones; to be human involves them all. This being true, it must be asserted that all are integrally related within the human experience of God. And the most sublime expression of this Divine/Human communion is found in worship. In worship we seek to express ourselves in relationship to God and to experience God's presence, individually and collectively.

As one who plans and leads Christian worship, I seek to be sensitive to the inter-relationships of intellect, feeling, and instinct in worship. I am convinced that good worship, whether public or private, will stretch the mind, move the heart, and gratify the senses. Poor worship is usually the result of the gross exaggeration of emphasis upon one of these aspects of human personhood. The believer should be challenged and given opportunity to experience the presence of God with every aspect of his/her personhood. The intellectual challenge of words, the emotional appeal of music, and the sensual appeal of visual art, ritual motion, religious symbols, liturgical garb, the taste and texture of the bread and the cup, the physical nearness of other human beings, and even the smells of candle smoke and incense are all important vehicles in mediating God's presence in worship.

Space does not permit the exploration of this line of thought in the context of the marketplace, the family, the arena of moral/ethical decision making, and other areas where we encounter, and are sometimes confronted by, God. However, if we remember that the distinction between sacred and secular is an artificial human distinction that often impedes more than it aids; it will not be difficult to apply the heads, hearts, and hormones insights related to worship to other aspects of our lives. In truth, if we properly inter-relate them in the experience of worship we are likely to find we are better able to inter-relate them in other areas as well. Worship is not a retreat from the realities of life; it is preparation for entry into them.

CHAPTER EIGHT
Piety Without Piousness

After a trying meeting with one of these people who are sure God has given them the last word on ultimate truth, my wife came home and said, "You know, some people are just too religious to do themselves or anyone else any good!" And I thought, "Sweetheart, you can say that again!" Many years ago I was both amused and convicted by the priceless piece of religious satire entitled, *How to be a Bishop Without Being Religious*. As a youthful minister I was challenged to avoid being caught up in the religious posturing that characterized many of my older contemporaries. By tone of voice, dress, and vocabulary they sought to exude an aura of holiness that set them apart from the ordinary run of human beings. Some of them possessed the gift of making the word "Gaaaaaaad" polysyllabic as they exhaled it with holy hoarseness.

Back in the 1960's and 1970's this phenomenon seemed primarily a preacher peculiarity. But the 1980's experienced more "trickle down" than in the economic realm, and today this malady has reached near epidemic proportions. I wonder if it's not time for a new work of religious satire. Perhaps this one could be called *How to be Religious Without Being a Pain in the Neck*.

Like so many things, today's problem of excessive religiosity is the product of good intentions gone astray. Rooted in the desire to genuinely reflect the qualities of God in one's life, the believer becomes excessively preoccupied with the external evidences of religious sincerity. Like the Pharisees of old, too much concern is focused upon the modern equivalent of the width of the hem of one's garments, or the legalistic tithing of insignificant quantities of unimportant commodities, or the holiness and sanctity of the expression on one's face. Jesus spoke sharply against this preoccupation with religious externals: "Woe to you, scribes and Pharisees, hypocrites! For you pay tithe of mint and anise and cumin, and have neglected the weightier matters of the law; justice and mercy and faith. These you ought to have done, without leaving the others undone" (Mt. 23:23 KJV). Herein lies the problem. It is not that one of these is important and the other unimportant. They are both important. The difficulty lies in relating them properly to one another. And our tendency is to focus upon the legalistic and ritualistic externals for two reasons: One, it is simpler and easier. And two, these externals are quantifiable in ways that make it possible for us to measure our success, and draw comparisons with our neighbors. But justice defies measurement by the pound. Mercy is not dispensed in gallons. And faith does not come in bolts to be cut off by the yard.

The contemporary challenge seems to be one of learning to exhibit genuine Christian *piety* without falling victim to self-righteous *piousness*. Before you conclude that this is simply a matter of mincing words, allow me to elaborate. While both these words have reference to the quality of religious life, the noun (*piety*) ordinarily refers to the reality and authenticity of such life, while the adjective (*piousness*) expresses the external appearance of religious authenticity not necessarily accompanied by any corresponding internal reality. Put more simply, *piety* most often refers to genuine Christian devotion, while *piousness* more commonly refers to religious affectation and pretense.

The question still remains, "How do we exhibit genuine *piety* without lapsing into legalistic, self-righteous *piousness*?" Perhaps scripture can offer some help. It often does, you know.

Exodus 20:1 – 17 finds the people of Israel standing before Moses to hear the content of *YHWH's* covenant expectations of them. This *Torah* (Law), known most commonly as The Ten Commandments, sets forth quite explicitly God's expectations for the people. While many think of this passage negatively, and hold that it is the basis of the very self-righteous legalism against which I am arguing, I beg to differ. I am prepared to assert that The Ten Commandments, read not as a list of legalistic rules, but as the practical foundation for appropriate human relationships, provides us with significant guidance regarding how we may reflect *piety* without affecting *piousness*.

Space does not permit a detailed analysis of Exodus 20 so, as much as I love and appreciate the value of such careful exegesis, I will restrain myself and concentrate upon three central principles that are relevant to *piety without piousness* in The Ten Commandments. The first principle is enshrined in the first two commandments focusing upon the uniqueness of God and the prohibition of idolatry. *Piousness*, in its negative sense, is usually the by-product of failing to remember that God is God, and you and I are not. From the biblical perspective, the core of human sinfulness is found in our tendency to reach beyond our creaturely createdness in the "image and likeness" of God, and appropriate the uniqueness of God for ourselves. The Genesis narratives of the Fall of Adam and Eve, and of Nimrod and the Tower of Babel, both emphasize the importance of maintaining the distinction between being "like" God and "being" God. Repeatedly, throughout the Old Testament, God reminded ancient Israel, "I am God, and you are not!"

This phenomenon is most often apparent today in the exercise of "playing God." While the phrase "playing God" is frequently used in reference to matters such as cloning, genetic engineering, euthanasia, abortion, environmental manipulation, and other significant biological and ethical issues, the term may also be used to refer to our interpersonal relations with others. We have moved beyond *piety* to *piousness* and are "playing God" when we appropriate God's role as judge for ourselves by condemning and excluding others because they think, or believe, somewhat differently than we do. We are "playing God" when we idolatrously set ourselves up as the standard by which the religious sincerity and righteousness of others is to be measured. We are "playing God" when we allow our egoistic need for praise and glory to seduce us into messianic pretentiousness as we present "ourselves" and "our way" as the solution to all problems. We cannot be reminded too often, "God is God, and we are not!" And we get into trouble every time we "play God."

A second principle is presented to us in Exodus 20:7 – 12. These commandments related to our use of language, our treatment of those who labor with us, and our reverence within the family remind us that respect for the personhood of others is the lubricant of all human relationships. It is often pointed out that one factor contributing to the upward spiral of violence in our society is the loss of civility in human interactions. Many of today's movies, sports figures, corporate executives, popular musicians, political aspirants, social activists, and even religious figures wholesale an "in-your-face" lack of civility devoid of any respect for the personhood of others, particularly those with whom they disagree or with whom they compete. And such behavior is not confined to the irreverence of TV sitcom characters, the bluster of professional wrestlers, or the rudeness of insulting and offensive bumper stickers. Many proponents of "Christian" religious values exhibit a shrill, vindictive intolerance of others that strips away personhood and leaves only ideological labels against which we rail: Fundamentalist! Liberal! Inerrantist! Secular Humanist! These labels become invectives, and the flesh and blood human beings we categorize with them are stripped of their personhood and reduced to disposable "things" that we may cast aside because we have concluded they are of no value to us. And the evidence that *piety* has descended into *piousness* is manifest in our attempts to disguise this disrespect and lack of civility toward others in so much self-righteous God-talk.

Third, the five *you shall nots* of Exodus 20:13 – 17 serve to keep us reminded that authentic religion is seen more in our *ethical* behavior than in our religious *airs*. While the quality of one's relationship to God should be characterized by much more than what one does not do, it still remains true that genuine religion will be reflected in the quality of the choices we make. It seems to me that *icthus* (fish) symbols and crosses on the bumpers of BMW, Lexus, and Mercedes-Benz automobiles, while the cost of one of these automobiles is greater than the gross lifetime income of most of the people who live on the planet, say more about religious *airs* than they do about Christian *ethics*. Billions spent by American congregations on elaborate and luxurious facilities devoted to the development of Christian "buns of steel" smack more of religious *airs* than Christian *ethics*.

The second half of The Ten Commandments asserts that authentic religion is reflected in reverence for life, marital fidelity, honesty, truthfulness, and goodwill toward others. Without these ethical qualities in our lives our religious observances, holy talk, Bible thumping, money giving, and symbol flashing are no more than religious *airs*, and are no different in kind than the religiosity of the Pharisees so sternly rebuked by Jesus. Now as then, when external appearance takes precedence over the quality of our moral/ethical decision making, our *piety* has become *piousness* and, in the words of Jesus, we are like whited sepulchers, filled with dead men's bones (Mt. 23:27).

What then are the identifying qualities of true Christian *piety*? Perhaps the scripture can help us once again. This time the answer may be found in Paul's advice to the Corinthian believers as they struggled to live with Christian authenticity in an environment that continually tempted them into artificiality and pretense. In a city given over to *eros*, the sensual, self-centered, egoistic, materialist manifestation of love that focuses upon getting and self-gratification, Paul pointed the Corinthians in the direction of *agape*, an others-centered love that deliberately lays aside impatience, envy, self-righteousness, and judgmentalism. In the midst of the Corinthian jangling, wrangling disputatiousness over who had the most desirable spiritual gifts, or the profoundest knowledge, or the greatest faith, or the most impressive good works, Paul spoke of a love that is never exhausted, an openness that is willing to grow, a maturity that is self-disciplining, and a hope that looks to the future.

Finally, it may be that the fullest expression of authentic Christian *piety* is to be found in the willingness to honestly acknowledge one's own spiritual limitations. Paul's "for now we see through a glass darkly," (I Cor. 13:12 KJV) is not an embracing of ignorance. Rather, it is an honest acknowledgment that we don't always know the right, or correct, or best answers; we don't always fully understand the implications of the challenge of the gospel for our lives; and we haven't fully fathomed the depths of what is means to know and be known by God.

But *piousness*, because it is rooted in pride, denies its own limitations and lack of insight, and does so by drawing attention to the limitations and failures of others. Insecure and unsure of itself, *piousness* must strut, and point, and pontificate. *Piousness*, forced to admit that it is not as good as God, insists, "While that may be true, I'm still better than you." *Piousness* mistakes *religiousness* for *holiness,* and in doing so gives authentic Christianity a bad name.

Piety without piousness, is it possible? Not completely between now and eternity. Honesty compels me to confess my own personal tendency toward *piousness* in the midst of my critique of this phenomenon. But hopefully, the sheer cultivation of the capacity to distinguish one from the other is movement in the right direction.

CHAPTER NINE
WWJD – Coping or Copping Out?*

I vividly recall the first time I saw a teen wearing a T-shirt emblazoned with the letters "WWJD". I thought she was a walking advertisement for a new radio or TV station. Later I learned the letters were an acrostic representing the question, "What would Jesus do?" Time passed and I observed this phenomenon as it spread across the American Christian community. The letters "WWJD" appeared on bracelets, bumper stickers, billboards, and banners all across the country. The more I saw of it, the more I wondered about this latest expression of what I sometimes call "pop" Christianity.

My theological training tells me the concerns expressed in the question, "What would Jesus do?" is neither unimportant nor new. A quick survey of classical Christian literature reveals that concern for living after the example of Jesus Christ was a primary preoccupation of the most spiritually insightful in the early Christian centuries. Apart from the New Testament literature, one needs only to mention the anonymously written *Shepherd of Hermas*, or the *Confessions* of Augustine of Hippo, or *The Imitation of Christ* by Thomas a Kempis to illustrate this point.

I am inclined to think today's phenomenon is yet another expression of the desire to be identified with Jesus Christ, this time filtered through the lens of 18th and 19th century Pietism as it has influenced the American Christian religious mentality. This yearning for spiritual renewal and guidance is to be found in Philip Jacob Spener's *Pia Desideria*, John Wesley's "Holy Club" at Oxford, Andrew Murray's books on prayer, and Charles M. Sheldon's *In His Steps*, to name only a few of the most widely known works and movements. More contemporary programs for spiritual growth such as *Renew* in Roman Catholic life and *MasterLife* and *Experiencing*

God in Southern Baptist circles reflect systematic and institutionalized forms of the desire to model one's behavior and decision-making after the example of Jesus Christ.

Not only is this sentiment not new, it is also not irrelevant. In the New Testament, the apostle Paul urged new believers to follow him as he sought to follow Christ (I Corinthians 4:16, 11:1; Philippians 3:17; I Thessalonians 1:6). We are told that early believers were first called *Christians*, meaning "little Christs," at Antioch in Syria (Acts 11:26). What was intended as an epithet of derision and ridicule, was turned by those earnest believers into a mark of personal identity with their Savior and Lord.

If all the above is true, what is it then that leaves me with a nagging uneasiness when I see the WWJD acrostic displayed so prominently? I suppose a part of it is the bracelets, bumper-stickers, billboards, and banners. Consistent Christian decision-making is demanding and difficult; it should never be trivialized. All the WWJD "hype," in my opinion, tends to submerge the Christian discipline and careful thinking necessary for good decision-making under a superficial veneer of marketing strategy. I am reminded of ads that imply that if I will only drink a particular product, I will lose weight; or if I drive the right automobile, I will be sexy; or if I have a particular credit card, I am financially responsible. While not denying the importance of the model of Jesus Christ as a guide, I would like to offer some cautions regarding the tendency toward simplistic responses to complex realities in contemporary Christian living and decision-making.

First, one of the major dangers in an uncritical emphasis upon the pietism of WWJD is its tendency toward excessive subjectivity. While the question, "What would Jesus do?" is a legitimate question, it can be used as a screen to disguise an over-emphasis upon self. We may end up using God-talk in order to imply that our primary focus is upon God, when, in truth, our major preoccupation is with ourselves. One of the besetting sins of much contemporary Christianity is its tendency to be excessively human-centered rather than God-centered. I may choose a dietary supplement, an automobile, or a credit card on the basis of "What's in it for me," but if my quest for the answer to the question, "What would Jesus do?" emerges from subjective self-interest, I have missed Jesus, the Man for Others, by my very pursuit of an answer to the question.

Second, in addition to its tendency toward subjectivity, the query, "What would Jesus do?" may beg the very question it asks. Truly the Christian is called to be Christ-like, but he or she is not called to *be* "Christ." The person Jesus of Nazareth who is the Christ is *sui generis* (one of a kind, unique). The Christian existential question is not primarily, "What would Jesus do?" Rather, it is, "On the basis of what God has done and continues to do in Jesus Christ, what should I do?" I hear much language that says, "Just turn your life over to Jesus and let God take care of everything." My reading of the New Testament suggests that when someone embraces Jesus Christ as Savior and Lord, God accepts, forgives, cleanses of sin, and gives the person right back to himself or herself with the command, "Now you live responsibly before me with this life." Certainly the "mind of Christ" (I Corinthians 2:16; Philippians 2:5) should inform our decision-making, but authentic Christian freedom maintains that our decisions are still *our* decisions.

Third, I suggest that an excessive emphasis upon WWJD tends toward a de-emphasis upon the *imago dei* (image of God) in all of us. The biblical revelation focuses upon the reality that human beings are created in the image and likeness of God for fellowship with the Divine. While the New Testament uses a variety of metaphors (putting on Christ, body of Christ, bride of Christ, and so forth) to point in the direction of the believer's identity with Christ, the emphasis is always upon identification with, not assimilation into. The Swiss theologian Karl Barth placed great emphasis upon, "the infinite, qualitative distinction between God and man." Put more simply, God is God and you and I are not. Contemporary Christian language often suggests a loss of individual personal identity as one is absorbed in God. Such assimilationist language sounds more like the *nirvana* of Hinduism than it does the "I and Thou" relationship of the Judaeo/Christian religious tradition.

A fourth caution in regard to an uncritical embracing of the WWJD mentality is that such an approach is often used to absolve one's self of responsibility for one's actions. We tend to avoid responsibility for bad judgment and poor decision-making by saying, "I meant well!" or "I was just doing what God told me to do!" Mature personhood, Christian or otherwise, requires that we take responsibility for our decisions and actions. Otherwise we lapse into a mentality of taking the credit when things go well, and giving "God" or "the Devil" the blame when they don't.

Finally, and perhaps most dangerously, once we have arrived at our answer to the question, "What would Jesus do?" in a given situation, we tend to want to universalize our conclusion and make it normative for everyone else. If we embrace this approach, the end result is a kind of lock-step Christian ethic in which right and wrong are determined by the viewpoint of the loudest or most persuasive exponent of our understanding of what Jesus would do in a specific situation. On the other hand, if we reject this lock-step uniformity and everyone embraces her or his own individual subjective understanding of WWJD, we end in an ethical relativism that concludes that something is "right" or "wrong" because the particular individual believes it is "right" or "wrong."

All five of these cautions may be summarized in the following: An uncritical embracing of WWJD does not take seriously enough the problem of human sinfulness. Because it does not adequately maintain the objective distinction between "what Jesus would do" and "what I (we) want to do," the simple query, "What would Jesus Do?" fails to be an effective guide for human decision-making.

Having said all of this, do not assume I am suggesting that Jesus provides the Christian with no model or guide for authentic decision-making. What I am suggesting is that we are better served if we look to the New Testament example of Jesus for overarching principles to guide our decision-making, rather than for legalistic rules regarding our behavior in specific instances.

When one looks at the New Testament record, certain principles are plainly evident. Among them are the following: (1) The actions of Jesus were consistent with the biblical revelation of God's overall purposes in creation and redemption. (2) Jesus valued persons above things. He never demeaned or depersonalized the men and women who were affected by his decision-making. (3) Jesus' actions were not self-aggrandizing. He was consistently "others"-centered rather than "self"-centered. (4) While not insensitive or uncaring about the thoughts of others, Jesus was willing to risk being misunderstood by others in order to be faithful to the will and purpose of God. (5) Jesus' actions appear to have been actuated by response to legitimate needs rather than by rigid obedience to a set of rules.

I am not implying that the above is an exhaustive list of the overarching principles that guided the decision-making and actions of Jesus.

I do, however, insist that these principles are a place to begin. They provide a matrix within which one may struggle to make one's own decisions, and then *own* the decisions one makes. They also provide a means to escape the inherent pride and presumption implicit in the suggestion that one may know exactly what Jesus would do in a specific contemporary decision-making situation. Quite frankly, I don't know what Jesus would do in certain situations. But I am convinced that whatever he would do would be God-oriented, person-affirming, others-centered, and need-sensitive. And I am convinced that he would embrace the responsibilities and risks inherent in his choices and deeds, rather than attempting to shift accountability for his actions onto someone else.

In this way the example of Jesus provides a model to help us cope with our own decision-making rather than "copping out" by claiming to let Jesus make the decision for us. The subjective emphasis upon exploring the question, "What would Jesus do?" ultimately ends in speculation. In the real world of complex decision-making in the present, there is no avoiding the question, "What will I do?" Hopefully, we will make God-oriented, person-affirming, others-centered, need-sensitive decisions in the context of real life and then, under God, *own* and live responsibly with our decisions and actions.

*Previously published in *Mature Years*, Fall, 2000.

CHAPTER TEN
Can a Little Heresy Be Good for Us?

One of my teachers would occasionally observe, "A heretic is a loser loser in a religious fight. And heresy is what the losing side believed." When I first heard them, these rather cynical words scandalized me. As a young minister, fresh out of college and in his early days of seminary training, I was so sure there was a simple, direct, certifiably correct answer to every question. Fearful of being wrong, I was determined to be absolutely orthodox in my beliefs and practices. And, honesty compels me to admit, I had little sympathy, and less tolerance, for those whose doctrinal purity did not measure up to my exacting standards. It is at this place that the words of Alexander Pope, in his *An Essay on Criticism*, need to be clearly heard:

> *A little learning is a dang'rous Thing;*
> *Drink deep, or taste not the Pierian Spring;*
> *There shallow Draughts intoxicate the Brain,*
> *And drinking largely sobers us again.* (Pt. 2, L. 15)

At about this time in my pilgrimage I spotted Paul Tillich's *A History of Christian Thought* on the bookshelf of a friend. Acquiring a copy of this work for myself, I carefully read it. Increasing acquaintance with the history of Christian theological reflection brought increasing awareness that most of the persons I wished to emulate as pillars of Christian doctrinal orthodoxy had, at one time or another, been condemned by someone as heretics.

Over the years my consciousness has been profoundly shaped by reading such seminal Christian thinkers as Origen, Athanasius, Augustine of Hippo, Thomas Aquinas, Peter Abelard, Erasmus of Rotterdam, Martin Luther, John Calvin, Roger Williams, Freidrich Schleiermacher, Rudolf

Bultman, Walter Rauschenbusch, Karl Barth, Emil Brunner, Pierre Teilhard de Chardin, Hans Kung, Rosemary Radford Reuther, Sallie McFague, Jurgen Moltmann, and many others. Growing familiarity with the lives and thought of these personalities revealed that each of them has, at one time or another, been accused and condemned for heresy, or had accused and condemned the heresy of others, or both. Along with this, a careful reading of the gospels made me acutely aware that the chief problem of the scribes and Pharisees with Jesus of Nazareth was what they perceived as his lack of religious orthodoxy.

By definition, heresy is false religious teaching, or doctrinal instruction that runs contrary to the generally accepted tenets of a particular religious system. In fact, more often than not, heresy is the result of taking a religious truth and pushing it too hard so that it becomes distorted and out of focus. As surely as artistic caricature is an exaggeration of visual reality, heresy is an exaggerated expression of religious truth. A typical illustration of such exaggeration is found in the ongoing Christian debate regarding the relationship of the divine and the human in the personhood of Jesus of Nazareth. Orthodox Christianity affirms that Jesus was both fully divine and fully human in dynamic relationship. Excessive emphasis upon the divine nature leads to a dismissal of his authentic humanity, and has been repeatedly judged heretical. Excessive emphasis upon the human nature leads to a denial of his divinity, and has been judged as equally heretical. This illustration serves to point out the primary danger in heresy. Heresy is not the absence of truth, but the distortion of it in one way or another, often by quite sincere persons for highly commendable reasons.

After more than a quarter of a century devoted to the systematic study of the history of Christian theological reflection, I have arrived at four conclusions. One, no one is absolutely right all the time. Two, very rarely is anyone absolutely wrong all the time. Three, the fact that a person is not right all the time does not mean that we cannot still learn from him or her. And four, a little heresy may be good for us.

It is with the fourth of these conclusions that I am primarily concerned at present. I repeat, "a little heresy may be good for us." Such an assertion demands and deserves some explanation. Thus, I will set forth the reasons why I am willing to embrace such a risky conclusion.

First, the sheer setting forth of religious beliefs held by others that are different from ours calls upon us to examine the integrity of our own beliefs. Much too often we believe what we believe simply because those beliefs have been inherited from our culture, and we have incorporated them into our world view without testing their validity against any objective standards. To Socrates is attributed the line, "The unexamined life is not worth living." I would concur with Socrates, and go on to add, "The unexamined faith is not worth having." Faith and reason are not polar opposites; they are siblings. Beliefs that run contrary to ours are of some value if they challenge us to examine the validity and trustworthiness of our own. In this way we are able to arrive at what Anthony Campollo has called, "A Reasonable Faith."

Second, beliefs that run contrary to our own may be of value if they serve as challenges to our self-righteousness. Here, once again, some words from Pope are valuable:

> *'Tis with our Judgments as our Watches, none*
> *Go just alike, yet each believes his own.*
> *(An Essay on Criticism,* Pt. 1, L. 9)

Often we begin a sentence with the words, "Well, I could be wrong . . . ." Usually this is the prelude to the immediate assertion that we don't think there is the remotest chance that we are.

I recall once being hotly challenged by a man who was sure I had done something I had not, in fact, done. When I suggested that he was operating under a mistaken assumption he asserted, with even more anger, "I don't make assumptions!" At this point I elected to end the discussion because his assumption that he didn't make assumptions was an assumption that I was not willing to assume was true. As long as he insisted upon operating from the position of, "Don't confuse me with facts; my mind's made up!" there was little point in my attempting to reason with him. It was clear, at least to him, that I must be wrong, because he couldn't possibly be.

Third, the challenge to examine our own beliefs in the context of assertions we think are false may lead us to the discovery of new insight. The 17th century near Pilgrim Father and proto-Baptist, John Robinson, preached on the wharf at Plymouth to the departing passengers of the *Mayflower*. In his farewell sermon Robinson said, "God yet has more truth and light to show forth from his holy word." Sometimes, in our zeal to understand and be right, we fail to realize that while we "get it" some of the time, we don't always "get it" all of the time, and we probably don't get "all of it" any of the time. In our concern for orthodoxy we should take care not to dismiss a new word from God as a false or heretical teaching simply because it is new to us, or it challenges long held presuppositions.

Fourth, when one's basic religious beliefs are challenged by confrontation with alternative belief systems, the end result can be the *owning* or internalizing of one's beliefs in a way that makes them infinitely more meaningful for us. As noted earlier, often we accept a pre-packaged body of religious beliefs from family, community, and culture without critically examining them. When this is the case our core beliefs are little more than social customs, superstitions, or prejudices. We believe the way we believe, and we behave the way we behave, for no more significant reason than that the people around us believe and behave in the same way and, in order to experience their acceptance and approval, we must conform to this pre-packaged belief system. It is only as we test our beliefs against alternative ways of understanding that they have any existential validity for us. Until this is done, our beliefs are always second hand; they belong to someone else, they are not our own.

Fifth, when we are forced to examine our own religious beliefs in the light of alternative beliefs, we may discover that it is we, not they, who are the heretics. Our inaccurate beliefs are not made true by frequent repetition. Our ill-formed beliefs are not made more true by being asserted at a louder volume. Our patently false beliefs are not even made true by pounding on a Bible and quoting scripture authoritatively. Sometimes we are just plain wrong, but we do not recognize our own error until confronted by another who sees and understands more clearly than we do. Thus, the one we presume to be an heretic sometimes, upon closer examination, turns out to be more orthodox than we are.

Finally, in the give and take of religious opinion, the process of learning to be more tolerant towards others who perceive differently than we do, and the willingness even to learn from them, can serve to keep us reminded that authentic *righteousness* is ultimately much more important than our own personal *rightness*. In the final analysis, it is not such a great thing to be right, when *rightness* is interpreted in terms of dominance, superiority, control, and the coercion of others to conform to our understanding of the truth. *Righteousness* is a divine quality that reflects the innermost character of God. *Rightness* is a preoccupation of the human ego which assumes that every question may be answered with mathematical precision, so that there is only one right or correct answer. It was this loss of distinction between *righteousness* and *rightness* that led John Calvin, the great Protestant Reformer, to consent to the death of Michael Servetus because Servetus would not conform to Calvin's understanding of the Doctrine of the Trinity. In my opinion, Calvin was theologically *right* in regard to his understanding of the Triune nature of God. However, it is also my opinion that Calvin demonstrated little God-like *righteousness* in his willingness to allow Servetus to be burned at the stake.

At this point you may assume I am advocating a kind of theological relativism that suggests "it doesn't matter what you believe as long as you're sincere." This is hardly the case. What I am asserting is that religious beliefs, most especially religious beliefs, must stand the test of the give and take of the marketplace of ideas. We must resist the temptation to embrace Tertullian of Carthage's stubborn, wrong-headed assertion, "I believe it because it is absurd." While much of the content of the Christian faith is non-rational in nature, it is not irrational. And there is nothing to be accomplished in pompously waving a Bible and self-righteously shouting, "God said it! I believe it! And that settles it!" This is inadequate for two reasons. First, if God has authentically said it, that settles it, whether you and I believe it or not. And second, neither you nor I are the last word on what God has said.

Ultimately, false religious teachings are not overcome by argumentative refutation. Too often when this is our approach we win the argument and lose the person. If it is true that the spirit of Christ is more caught than taught, then the real test of the authenticity of our doctrinal assertions is reflected in the Christ-like character of our lives.

If my teacher is correct in his assertion that orthodoxy is often no more than a reflection of the opinion of the most powerful, or the most persuasive, or the most numerous, then it may be that the occasional heretic is a gift from God. For these minority voices challenge our complacency and force us to examine the validity of our religious assertions. They remind us that the majority is not always correct; it is only the majority. Authentic truth has a persuasiveness about it that, over time, will ultimately prevail. And the passage of time often reveals that one era's heretic is another era's saint.

CHAPTER ELEVEN
The Gospel According to Woodworkers

Some years ago a good friend drew me into the sub-culture of wood workers by offering to guide me through the process of building a coffee table and end tables as a wedding present for my son and his bride. It turned out that not only did I not cut off any body parts; I also had something of a knack for working with tools. Before I realized it I was hooked; I had sawdust in my veins. That initial project was followed by more tables, a small desk, a blanket chest, an entertainment center, a china cabinet, several kitchen islands, a buffet server, book-cases, and a grandfather clock. Now I read woodworking magazines, bore my friends and neighbors talking about my projects, and go into withdrawal symptoms if too many days pass without spending some time in my shop.

It did not take long to discover there are certain basic truths associated with woodworking. One such truth is the importance of keeping one's tools sharp and well adjusted. This should be done for two reasons: first, one is less likely to get hurt if the tools are properly cared for and, second, the materials are less likely to be damaged by sharp, well adjusted tools.

Another axiom observed by all serious woodworkers is the importance of knowing and respecting the materials with which one works. Only a little experience demonstrates to the novice woodworker that one piece of wood is not the same as another. Each medium (pine, oak, mahogany, cedar, cypress, hickory, birch, poplar, walnut, pecan, etc.) has its own grain pattern, hardness, tendency to warp or split, and many other characteristics. All respond differently to the application of tools. Some are easily worked by hand; others defy being shaped by anything other than the strongest of power tools. Knowledge of and respect for the

61

material one works with is essential to good craftsmanship.

Perhaps the best know truism of woodworkers is the old saw (pun intended) "measure twice, cut once." Closely akin to this is the importance of using the same measuring instrument throughout a project. Everyone has a story of how an expensive piece of material was wasted because someone was not careful to measure exactly, resulting in a board being cut too short. All serious woodworkers understand that it is virtually impossible to keep a project plumb and square if you do not use the same measuring instrument each time. What appear to be minute differences in calibration on measuring tapes or tri-squares can turn out to be major differences when projected over distances.

Any good woodworker will also counsel, "Take your time; never work when you are tired." Hurry and fatigue are the greatest enemies of fine craftsmanship. Both contribute to concentration errors where the craftsman makes unnecessary mistakes because he or she is too tired or too hurried to focus effectively. In addition, hurry and fatigue are just plain dangerous. Even a casual survey of woodworkers who have sustained injuries while working in their shops will reveal that accidents and injuries are most often the consequence of carelessness resulting from fatigue and/or hurry. Besides, if you cannot take time to savor the process of designing and building, much of the joy of working on a project is lost.

Finally, all good craftsmen will tell you that the project isn't finished until you have cleaned up the shop and put away your tools. There is a kind of psychological closure that accompanies the ritual of cleaning up and putting away. The mind is able to step back, contemplate, savor, and appreciate. For most of us, the nature of the work we do provides minimal opportunity to experience the satisfaction derived from completing a task and knowing that it has been done well. Such closure makes it possible, after a rest, to begin to envision, plan, and execute the next project.

In my more reflective moments I am inclined to think there are many analogies between fine woodworking and the process of spiritual growth and development in the Christian believer's life. Much of what is true about woodworking is also true about disciplined, maturing Christian faith. Take, for instance, the woodworker's axiom related to the importance of keeping one's tools sharp and well adjusted. One of the greatest deterrents to real spiritual development is the tendency of many Christians to be careless with their spiritual gifts. Through mental laziness, mistaken assumptions, and undisciplined attitudes we allow our capacities for real discernment, sound judgment, and mature action to become dull and ineffective. The end result is often injury, both to ourselves and to others. There is little use in possessing the "breastplate of righteousness, the shield of faith, and the sword of the spirit," (Eph. 6:14-17) if the breastplate is tarnished and rusty, the shield is dented and broken, and the sword is dull. It is incumbent upon every Christian to keep his/her prayer life up to date. There is no excuse for ignorance of biblical content on the part of people who consider themselves to be literate and reasonably well educated. Many professions decline to re-certify practitioners who refuse or neglect to stay current in their callings. Unfortunately, within the Christian community we appear to have concluded that marginal biblical competency and casual Christian conduct are not only acceptable, but commendable.

Like woodworkers, Christians need to know and respect the materials with which they work. These materials are essentially two in number: the content of the gospel message, and the lives of those to whom we minister. The essential core of the gospel message is continually in danger of becoming encrusted with baggage drawn from culture, society, custom, bad habits, false teachings, etc. that are not a part of the gospel. The very fact that the gospel must be proclaimed within the world means it can never be kept completely separate from these cultural and social accretions. However, it is absolutely important that those entrusted with bearing witness to the gospel know the difference between "gospel" and "cultural accretions."

Perhaps an analogy from woodworking will illustrate the point. The trunk of every tree consists of three types of material: bark, sapwood, and heartwood. Bark is essentially useless in woodworking. Sapwood tends to be uneven in grain, color, texture, and strength. All good craftsmen know that fine furniture can be made only from the heartwood. Sectarianism, denominationalism, Christianity so mixed with political agendas it is difficult to tell one from the other, and other social and cultural accretions are like the bark and sapwood. While they are inevitabilities, they are not the gospel. And a Christian who cannot tell the difference between the heartwood of the gospel and the social/cultural sapwood and bark surrounding it endangers himself and others by preaching a message of enslaving conformity to the mores and values of a particular sub-group, instead of proclaiming a message of liberating transformation that results from being encountered by the living God.

Christians should also know the people to whom they are proclaiming the gospel. While all of us share a common humanity and, in our fallenness, stand in need of redemption and restoration to a right relationship with God, individual human beings and people groups are not identical to one another. We are conditioned and shaped by environment, genetics, education, life experience, age, gender, ethnicity, and many, many other factors. The end result is that our thought processes, our needs, our ways of experiencing are different. And a "once size fits all" proclamation of the gospel strips away the uniqueness of each person's humanity. While it is true that there is "one Lord, one faith, one baptism, one God and Father of all, who is above all and through all and in all . . ." (Eph. 4:5-6), it is also true that "each of us was given grace according to the measure of Christ's gift" (Eph. 4:7). If you want composite, pressboard, mass produced furniture go to Wal-Mart, K-Mart, Home Depot, or Lowes. If you want fine, custom built furniture, find a first-class craftsperson and let them build it for you. To say Christ died for all of us is also to say Christ died for each of us. And the gospel is not about stamping out stereotyped, composite, pressboard religious clones; it is about reaching and redeeming each man, each woman, and each child as the unique persons they are. And those outside the Christian community are right when they say, "If you want to reach me, take the time to care enough to get to know me."

Earlier I mentioned how important it is for the woodworker to be exactingly careful in making measurements, and to insure accuracy by using the same measuring instrument each time. The analogy here needs little elaboration. There is only one standard by which Christian authenticity may be appropriately measured; it is the standard of Jesus Christ. One of my teachers used to say, "If you want to know what God is like, look to how God has revealed Himself in Jesus Christ. And if you want to know what God wants you to be like, look to how God has revealed Himself in Jesus Christ." Within the Christian community we spend too much time and energy making sidelong comparative glances at one another. We often say, "I'm as good as Bill," or "I'm more faithful than Jane," or "I wish I were more like Tommy." Despite the qualities we may deplore or admire in Bill and Jane and Tommy, Bill and Jane and Tommy are not the ultimate standard by which our Christian maturity is to be measured. Paul told the Galatian Christians, "I have been crucified with Christ; and it is no longer I who live, but it is Christ who lives in me" (Gal. 2:20). The author of I Timothy said, ". . . there is . . . one mediator between God and humankind, Christ Jesus . . ." (I Tim. 2:5). If we are careful to measure by the standard of Christ Jesus we will never mar, or damage, or waste the lives God has entrusted to our care.

As surely as hurry and fatigue are the great enemies of the woodworker's craft, so impatience and weariness are the great enemies of those who would cooperate with God in what God is doing in the world. God reminded the people of Israel, "my thoughts are not your thoughts, nor are your ways my ways . . ." (Is. 55:8). Repeatedly the scripture speaks of what God brings about in the "fullness of time." Paul encouraged the Galatians, "Let us not be weary in well doing for in due season we shall reap, if we faint not" (Gal. 6:9).

From the opening chapters of the Bible through to its closing verses, the relationship between creativity and rest are emphasized. Life is lived in the appropriate tension between activity and rest. The heart that beats frenetically will die. The heart that never beats is already dead. Where there is a balanced tension between work and rest there is life. And the Christian who announces piously, "I'll rest when I get to heaven!" may be guilt of thinking "more highly of himself than he ought to think . . ." (Rom 12:3).

Finally, Christians, like woodworkers, should cultivate the capacity to step back, contemplate, savor, and appreciate. The joy, well-being, celebration, and sense of accomplishment in Christian living are all far too important to put off "till we all get to heaven." Heaven, the fullness of fellowship in the presence of God, is not just then and there; it is also here and now. And while it is true that what we can experience here and now is only a foretaste of what God ultimately has in store, there is no reason to deny ourselves the joy of the present. So periodically we should step back, clean up and take inventory of our lives, savor and be grateful for how far we have come in the journey toward Christ-likeness, and then move on to whatever is next. To use another analogy, part of the thrill of climbing a mountain is the joy of pausing to contemplate the view along the way.

CHAPTER TWELVE
Why Have a Pool if You Never Go for a Dip?

Anumber of years ago my wife and I bought a modest house in the Rutherford County community of Shingle Hollow. The previous owner had installed an in ground swimming pool on the property as a place for his wife, who had terminal cancer, to exercise during the last years of her declining health. Peggy and I were attracted by the floor plan and condition of the house, the property surrounding it, and the splendid mountain views in the area. Since neither of us is a serious swimmer, the pool was only an incidental attraction. We would have bought the house and property even if there had been no swimming pool. Subsequently we have closed the pool and are in the process of having it filled in.

The first year or two our then teenaged sons, especially the younger one, were thrilled with owning a backyard pool. It was a place for parties with their high school and college friends, and a middle-class status symbol they found attractive. Time soon demonstrated they were less enamored with cleaning, vacuuming, chemically treating, and seasonally opening and closing it. After they left home, their mom and I were left with a pool that, for some years, we dutifully cleaned and cared for each summer in anticipation of the occasional visits from the boys and their families. The children and grandchildren would cavort briefly in the pool, and then move on to other things. And I would find myself musing on the prospect of having the pool filled in, and building myself a woodworking shop in its place. While one part of my mind did such self-interested musing, another part would say, "Well, when the grandchildren are older they may want to use the pool more;" or "After Peg and I retire, we will have more time to use it;" or "If we decide to put the house on the market, the pool might be a good selling point." While such rationalizations may have been correct, all these hopes lay out there in the relatively distant and indistinct future. They still did not address my present tense question, "Why have a pool if you never go for a dip?"

In my more philosophical moments, I have reflected upon the Gregg's pool as a parable of life in general. We have so much that we never use with any degree of disciplined seriousness. Here I speak not so much of material possessions, of which most Americans have a super-abundance, but of less tangible possessions. Among these I would number our mental capacities, our faith, our ability to express and live in loving relationships, our talents and skills, and our capacity for hope.

As a confessing Christian who considers himself both a thinking believer and a believing thinker, I am particularly troubled by the tendency of so many of us to let others do our thinking for us, and by our tendency to live on second hand faith. This leaves many of us acknowledging, without meaning to, that "I have a brain, I just don't use it very much." And "I know that as a Christian I believe some things, but I'm not really sure what those beliefs are or why I hold them." The end result is that most of our living and decision-making is done on the basis of inadequate reason and insecure faith.

One of the more troubling phenomena of contemporary life is the tendency toward excessive dependence upon charismatic personalities to do our thinking for us. Often we blame this abandonment of personal intellectual responsibility upon the complexity of life in a modern techno-logical society. While there is no denying that we live in a more complex world than previous generations, it is not a logical corollary that Regis Philbin, or Oprah Winfrey, or Rush Limbaugh, or anyone else is more intelligent than most of the rest of us; or that Tom Hank's or Sybil Shepherd's or Jerry Falwell's moral and social discernment is superior to that of oth-ers; or, for that matter that Franklin Graham's or Charles Stanley's God consciousness is greater than mine or yours. While celebrity status is not devoid of intellectual, spiritual, or cultural insight, it is also not synonymous with these characteristics. And if I arrive at a particular conclusion for no more significant reasons than that Oprah, or Rush, or Franklin said so, then I have surrendered my capacity to think for myself and am allowing Oprah, or Rush, or Franklin to do my thinking for me. It matters not whether Oprah, or Rush, or Franklin is correct or incorrect. My guess is that, like the rest of us, they are sometimes correct and sometimes incorrect; sometimes they think with objective clarity and sometimes their judgment is clouded by sentiment, or ego, or prejudice, or personal dislike. What does matter is the capacity to sort through the data, arrive at a decision based upon one's best understanding of the information available, and the courage to accept responsibility and live with the consequences of the decisions one makes. If incidentally, one's conclusions are the same as those of Oprah, or Rush, or Franklin that's fine. I would hope that my conclusions are, more often than not, similar to those of other mature, rational people. But I still want those conclusions to be my conclusions arrived at by the responsible use of my own capacity to think and decide.

A second, equally troubling phenomenon, particularly from the perspective of religious beliefs, is the tendency of so many to trust in second-hand faith. Admittedly, most of us absorbed many of our most basic religious insights and values from the religious-cultural environment in which we were nurtured. We embraced or rejected the faith affirmations of our families, our communities, and our nation. This is natural and to be expected.

I am a Christian by confession and a Baptist by denominational tradition. But I must admit that, at least to some degree, I embraced Christianity as a young teenager because during a time of personal crisis it was the only religious option available. Further, I became a Baptist because it was the dominant expression of Christianity in the West Alabama environment in which I grew up. While I remain unapologetically both Christian and Baptist, I like to think my reasons for remaining so are much more carefully thought out than my original reasons for becoming either Christian or Baptist.

I suspect I am neither the first nor the last believer to face the reality that for a long time he/she lived on borrowed, second-hand faith affirmations that were fervently repeated but never critically examined or maturely reflected upon. Further, I am convinced that the Apostle Paul was one of our company as well, and I find much encouragement in his willingness to acknowledge that "when I was a child, I spoke like a child, I thought like a child, I reasoned like a child . . ." (I Cor. 13:11a NRSV). Here I chime in, "Me too!" But in the next breath he said, "when I became an adult, I put an end to childish ways" (I Cor. 13:11b NRSV). And here I am challenged to declare, "I will too!"

In what may legitimately be called the first Christian tract, the New Testament writer, Jude, urged his readers to "contend for the faith that was once for all entrusted to the saints . . ." (Jude 3 NIV). His occasion for writing seems to be that, with the passage of only a few decades, second generation Christians were in danger of being led astray by false teachers because of their failure to personally own and internalize the body of beliefs that had been passed on to them from the original followers of Jesus. This is always the danger in excessive dependence upon "what mom and dad taught me," or "what the preacher said," or "what I've always been told was true," or some other variation of the whining admission that we have been letting others do our thinking and believing for us. Because we have failed to reverently and critically examine and test our beliefs, we are often easily led astray by those who appeal to our sentimentalism, or who speak with an authoritative tone, or who eagerly volunteer to do our thinking for us.

By now it should be apparent that this little exercise in reflective thinking has almost nothing to do with the Gregg's backyard pool. After all, in the final analysis, that is just a hole in the ground with water in it. The real challenge is to honestly face the reality that brains are for thinking, and faith is for living. If it is reasonable to assume that people who have a pool should swim in it, it is equally reasonable to assume that people with brains and faith should think carefully and live faithfully.

People who have pools should also have some rules governing their appropriate use. At the Gregg house these included things like never leaving the fence gate open and the pool unattended, and never swimming alone. Such rules were intended to protect the lives of the Greggs and their guests, as well as neighbors and friends. Thinking believers and believing thinkers need to have some foundational principles that guide the use of their brains and the exercise of their faith as well. It is my opinion that any such list of principles should include the following:

First, love and trust yourself at least as much as God does. We have been culturally and religiously conditioned to downplay our capacity to think and act responsibly in our world. This runs contrary to God's expressions of trust for human beings, even in their fallenness. The central unifying reality of Christianity is the event of the Incarnation/Resurrection of Jesus Christ. In the Incarnation God said to humankind, "I love and trust you enough to become like you." In the Resurrection God said,

70

"Now, you love and trust me enough to become like me." The Christian understanding of the Church as the Body of Christ is witness to the belief in the continuation of the Incarnation in the lives and actions of people on their way to Resurrection. If it is true that the believer should love God because God first loved us, it is equally true that the believer should trust God because God has trusted, and continues to trust, us.

Second, remember that faith, genuine Christian faith, is not a blind leap, but an expression of insight-filled trust. Such faith does not require that we turn off our capacity to reason and think carefully. On the contrary, such faith demands that we reason and think carefully. Listen to the cadences of rational reflection and insight-filled trust in the confession of the biblical writer that "I *know* the one in whom I have *put* my trust, and am *sure* that he is able to guard . . . *what I have entrusted* to him" II Tim. 1:12 NRSV, *Italics* mine).

Third, if you must make a choice between courage and caution, err or the side of courage. The Christian faith is not a religion of the faint of heart. Jesus demanded of his first disciples that they risk everything in order to follow him. He demands no less of you and me. Courage is not the absence of fear; courage is the act of taking the risks inherent in faith even though one is afraid. Having faith in God does not mean that everything is going to turn out just the way we want it to. Having faith in God means that we are sure God will be with us not matter how things turn out.

And finally, remember that *CREDO* means *I believe."* Put more literally it means, "*I* have become convinced." Convictions are, by definition, not blindly and uncritically held assertions, but conclusions arrived at through careful examination and reflection. Such beliefs/convictions are firmly held only in the first person singular; they are never attainable if they have simply been borrowed uncritically from others. It is one thing to hold a body of beliefs in common with others; it is another to subscribe to a body of beliefs simply because others do. So, why have a pool if you never go for a dip? And why have a brain if you are going to let others do your thinking for you? And, why have faith if you are not going to live courageously with insight-filled trust? You can ignore questions such as these, but they won't go away.

CHAPTER THIRTEEN
The Cloning of Christians –
To Be Like Jesus Is To Be Like Me

The sincere Christian who takes his/her responsibility to "be . . . an example of the believers, in word, in conversation, in charity, in spirit, in faith, in purity" (I Tim. 4:12) is caught on the horns of a dilemma. On the one hand, all of us need role models and we are role models for others. The New Testament writers recognized this truth (Heb. 4:11; Ja. 5:10). Repeatedly Paul cautioned his readers to take care in how they lived because others within the community were observing and imitating their behavior (Rom. 14:13, 21; I Tim. 4:12; Titus 2:7). In more than one place the Apostle to the Gentiles called upon others to follow him as he followed Jesus (I Cor. 4:16; Phi. 3:17; II Th. 3:7-9; II Tim. 1:13).

On the other hand, our human propensity to self-centered sinfulness can lead us to take our role modeling responsibility entirely too seriously. When we do so we often make ourselves the ideal standard of what it means to be a faithful follower of Jesus Christ. Once we have arrived at this place, it is only one more short step to judging the authenticity of the Christian experience of others on the basis of how "like" or "unlike" us they are. At this point we have adopted a stance that says, "to be like Jesus is to be like me." And its unfortunate corollary is the conclusion that "if you're not like me, then you're not like Jesus."

In recent decades I have witnessed the simultaneous manifestation of two phenomena in the life of the contemporary Christian community. One of them is the development of the mega-church and its accompanying ministerial model of the pastor as CEO or Chairman of the Board of the congregation. The other, a by-product of the influence of mass

72

media upon American religious culture, is the emergence of charismatic religious personalities who, primarily through the skillful use of television, exert inordinate amounts of influence upon the thinking and actions of their followers. Both these phenomena have contributed significantly to an excessive emphasis upon the personal appeal and influence of pivotal individuals. The end result is that many religious communities have been reduced to little more than cults of personality. And, in its most dangerous manifestations, these magnetic personalities take on messianic pretensions, and their need to be emulated drives them to set themselves up as paradigms of the ideal Christian role model. Their central message is "to be like Jesus is to be like me!" Worship, Christian education, the founding of colleges and seminaries, and the conducting of endless seminars are designed to foster the cloning of followers who believe, think, vote, dress, and live after the model of the central personality.

The challenge before the contemporary Christian leader, whether minister or layperson, is the appropriate stewardship of one's role modeling responsibility. The aim is to develop the skills necessary to positively influence and mentor others without permitting one's ego needs to lead to the abuse of the power and trust others invest us with. One is less likely to fall victim to the temptation to abuse one's power over others by keeping in mind a few basic biblical insights.

First, the biblical account of creation emphasizes that human beings are created in the image (*selem*) and likeness (*demuth*) of the Creator. While time does not allow, and I lack the insight, to explore all it means for human beings to be created like God, there is one truth that is clear from the creation narrative. God is not some "thing" but Someone; God is Divine Person, not an object. To be created in the divine image and likeness, at least, emphasizes that human beings are "persons" and not "things." Thus, in our relations with others, appropriate attention should be given to their personhood. Any attitude or action on our part that robs another of personhood and reduces her/him to a mere object for our manipulation and control is inappropriate on the part of the Christian leader.

Second, the creation narrative emphasizes the otherness of God from the created order. God is seen as the "One who causes to be" and the created order, including human beings, is that which has been "caused to be." Creator and created exist in dynamic relationship, but they are not identical with one another. This is a useful insight to keep in mind in our relations with others. While our corporate identity as human beings emphasizes the dynamic relationship we share with other persons, individual autonomous personhood is not swallowed up in corporate identity. As surely as the vertical reality of our "I-Thou" relationship to the Creator must not be lost; it is also true that, horizontally, we live in "I-Thou" relationships with others. And as leaders and role models we must understand that no approach that diminishes the autonomous personhood of "Thou" in order to subjugate and absorb into "I" is acceptable. As surely as the dynamic tension between "Creator" and "created" is fundamental to a biblical understanding of the relationship between God and the created order, the dynamic tension between "self" and "others" is fundamental to a biblical understanding of authentic personhood. While "I" am not alone, I am also not "Legion."

A third insight, while rooted in the biblical literature, is also an historical reality. It is the truth that persons who have claimed identity with the God of the Judaeo/Christian religious tradition have never been universally homogenous in their understanding and/or practice. Diversity of experience, changing historical circumstances, cultural infiltration, differing interpretations of divine disclosure, and, without doubt, sheer human "onoriness" have all influenced the shape of Judaeo/Christian history. While some of this diversity may be rightly attributable to heretical (false) religious beliefs and teachings, much of it is the simple, wonderful, and not to be minimized by-product of the richness and grandeur of both divine revelation and human insight.

The multiplicity of divine names in the Old Testament (*El* - Divinity, *El-Elyon* – God Most High, *El-Olam* – Everlasting God, *El-Shaddai* – Almighty, *Abir* – Mighty One, *Pahad* – Fear, *Elohim* – God, *Adonai* – Lord, *Yahweh* – I AM) should serve to keep us reminded of the diversity of the patriarchs' and matriarchs' experience with, and understanding of, God. The fact that God appeared to Abraham, Isaac, and Jacob as *El-Shaddai* (Ex. 6:3), to Moses as *Yahweh* (Ex. 3:14), and to Isaiah as *Adonai* (Is. 6:1-13) diminishes neither the authenticity nor the quality of each man's encounter with the Divine One. Yet it does emphasize two things: First, the reality of God is too vast to be summarized and captured in a single name. Second, the experience of God is conditioned by the circumstances and needs of the personality to whom God is disclosing the Divine Self. It is both a Divine/Human, and a Human/Divine encounter.

When this understanding is combined with the diversity between Hellenists and Judaizers, Paul and Simon Peter, Synoptic writers and the Johannine tradition, Roman Catholics and Protestant Reformers, etc. one should conclude that authentic Christian experience does not require monolithic orthodoxy. In truth, diversity of understanding and interpretation has been more norm than idiosyncrasy and aberration across the centuries of Christian history. *Heterodoxy* (diversity of belief) and *heresy* (false belief), while related, are not synonymous. Sometimes it is good for us to recall the pointed insight of Bishop William Warburton that "Orthodoxy is my doxy, heterodoxy is another man's doxy." At least it will help keep us from taking ourselves too seriously when we are reminded that God cannot, and will not, be contained in anyone's *doxy*.

Over the years church members, students, fellow ministers, and total strangers have asked, "Dr. Gregg, what do you believe about . . . ?" or "Do you believe in . . . ?" On such occasions I have always tried to help the questioner learn to use language more precisely. Effective use of language may be the best corrective to the modern tendency to assume that mentoring and providing a role model for others means molding them into exact copies of ourselves.

One of the first lessons in the proper use of language is the recognition that we often get into trouble if we use phrases interchangeably when it would be better to distinguish them. For instance, frequently someone will use the phrase, "I believe," and the phrase , "I think," to express precisely the same sentiment. The danger in this careless use of language is its tendency to confuse "articles of faith" with "opinion" and "personal point of view."

When dealing with issues of religious conviction and orthodoxy the phrase, "I believe," should be reserved for articles of faith, or to use an old Reformation concept, those beliefs upon which the standing or the falling of the faith are dependent. I am convinced the Christian use of the word "believe" should be limited to a rather short confessional list, and that this list is summarized in the ancient confession that has come to be called the "Apostle's Creed." When one seeks to define the core of Christianity, these basic beliefs are non-negotiable. To eliminate any one of them detracts from the Christian understanding of what God has done, and continues to do, in and through Jesus Christ.

On the other hand, there are biblical concepts that, while not irrelevant, are not at the core of understanding the Divine redemptive disclosure. To use another Reformation expression, these are *adiaphora*, things indifferent. Among such things I would include obsessive concern over the length of a person's hair, where Cain got his wife, and even, dare I say it, whether the "Second Coming" will take place before or after the "Great Tribulation."

The maturing Christian is called upon to be both a believing thinker and a thinking believer. In order to do so one must differentiate between core beliefs that are basic to the definition of what it means to be a Christian, and other matters that, while not inconsequential, are not core beliefs. Thus I *believe* in God the Father Almighty, maker of heaven and earth . . . ." While I may give careful thought to the implications of this, and other articles of the Apostle's Creed, I do so through the lens of *credo ut intelligam*, "I believe in order that I may understand." In addition, I also *think* carefully about certain social and moral issues, matters of controversy, political positions, economic systems, etc. But I never say such things as, "I *believe* or don't *believe* in evolution," or "I *believe* that the Marxist view of economics is of the devil" or "I *believe* that capital punishment is wrong." In instances such as these I say, "I *think* that this is true or untrue," or "The evidence I have access to at this time seems to indicate," or "It is my strongly held opinion that this, or that, is the right position."

It is here that the Christian leader may exert his/her influence as mentor and role model without insisting that the only truth that exists is, "The truth as I see it." By learning to use language appropriately it is possible to stand firmly upon convictions that are considered to be non-negotiable without allowing ego, and the need always to be right, to turn us into ideologues. We are able to shape and mold, influence and disciple, while allowing others to retain the full measure of their own Christian personhood. The end result is the production of thoughtful, reflective believers who have wrestled with and owned their convictions in the midst of the crucible of life.

The church of the 21st century does not need clones who, automaton like, merely mimic and parrot the actions and words of some overpowering human personality. And it has no need for megalomaniacs who insist upon controlling the lives of people who come under their influence. The church of the 21st century needs men and women who will "love the Lord [their] God with all [their] heart, and with all [their] soul, and with all [their] mind . . ." and who will "love [their] neighbor as [themselves]" (Mt. 22:37, 39). In doing so we can lay aside an attitude that communicates that "to be like Jesus is to be exactly like me." Instead we can embrace a way of relating that says, "to be like Jesus is to be like Jesus."

CHAPTER FOURTEEN
Darn the Yellow Jackets:
The Grass Still Has to Be Mowed

It was one of those almost unbearably hot late July afternoons in Western North Carolina. For weeks the sun had unrelentingly scorched the earth until the leaves drooped listlessly on the trees, birds seemed to fly and chirp no more than absolutely necessary, and grass mowing was down to every other week.

It is a matter of some pride to my wife that our acre and a quarter in the foothills of the Blue Ridge be well trimmed for the benefit of passersby on the paved country road that meanders past the front of our place. Therefore, I had received my orders before she left for work that morning. The scrubby dandelions and various other weeds that still managed to grow, even though the grass had long since gone into dormancy, needed to be mowed. So, that sweltering afternoon I got out the old push mower and went to work on the front "lawn." Actually it is a front yard. I have better things to do with both my time and my money than waste either on cultivating a lawn.

I had been mowing for less than half an hour when, with absolutely no warning, a sharp, stinging pain on the top of my right hand shocked me into releasing the throttle control on the mower. Before I had time to realize what was happening, a second yellow jacket torpedoed the back of my neck. As I fled shamelessly from the onslaught, a third of these savage monsters injected its venom into the calf of my left leg. Thinking thoughts that are unmentionable, I crashed through the back door and into the den, limping from the injury to my leg, and already sensing the swelling of my hand and neck. I needed cold relief immediately, and I was wounded in too many places for a simple cube of ice. Running through the house, shedding clothes as I ran, I leaped into the shower and twisted the faucet, cold water only. The shock of the icy cold water from our almost fathomless deep well forced a primal grunt from me, but the cold was preferable to the pain. For several minutes I stood beneath the needling stream of cold mountain water, allowing it to drain the pain and heat from my hand and neck and leg.

Emerging from the shower, I dried gingerly and, after dressing in denim cutoffs and a loose fitting golf shirt, I walked back through the house, gathering up the sweaty working clothes I had abandoned so haphazardly a few minutes before. Passing through the kitchen, I helped myself to two extra-strength Excedrin. Then I returned to the den, ensconced myself in my favorite recliner, let Clancy, our Yorkshire Terrier, curl up in my lap, and settled down for a nap. My next-to-the-last though was, "Darn the yellow jackets!" And then remembering my wife's instructions, my last thought was, "That grass still has to be mowed."

Years ago Dolly Parton sang, *Life is Like a Butterfly*. I suppose the images she had in mind as she wrote those poetic lyrics included change, fragility, beauty, and elegance. Life is also like a weed-infested front yard with a yellow jacket hole in the middle of it. Though this image is much more prosaic, one cannot deny that life is also characterized by the mundane, ugly, painful, and ridiculous. In fact, real life is lived in the nexus where these two sets of images converge. Authentic life is never "this" or "that." It is always "this and that" inextricably mixed together. While we prefer to dwell upon the more positive and aesthetically pleasing aspects of the butterfly image, there are useful things to be learned from reflecting upon the reality of the yellow jackets as well.

Almost all creatures, when threatened, or when they perceive they are threatened, will defend themselves. This is true with yellow jackets. It is also true of human beings. In this instance, I had no intention of doing harm to the yellow jackets. I only wanted to cut the grass. Often we have no intention of doing harm to others. However, they perceive that we are a threat to their way of life, sense of importance, means of earning a living, or their very existence. Under this impression, they move to eliminate us before we eliminate them. In human relations we are sometimes stung, or we sting others, by venomous falsehood, betrayal, verbal abuse, and, on occasion, even physical violence. Sometimes these actions are premeditated and malicious. Often they are no more than instinctive reaction to a perceived threat from another. But, whether premeditated or unintentional, the injury and pain experienced is no less real.

Thus it is important that people remember they are human beings, not yellow jacks. While one cannot fault the yellow jacket for reacting on nothing more than its instinctive need for survival, human beings should expect more, and deserve more, from one another.

Consciousness of self and one's own needs implies the capacity for awareness of others and their needs as well. Human beings are capable of thinking, evaluating, and choosing, and thus, are capable of arriving at conclusions and choosing actions based upon more than instinct and self-interest. "Do unto others before they have a chance to do unto you" may be a fundamental law of random natural selection and the survival of the fittest; but all human religious, aesthetic, philosophical, and moral insight calls us to a higher norm in relationship with others. Whether we look to the maxim of Israel's ancient sages as reformulated in Jesus' Golden Rule, "do unto others as you would have them do unto you," or to its philosophical expression in Immanuel Kant's Categorical Imperative, "act in no way you are not at the same time willing to universalize;" deeply embedded in human consciousness there is an inherent awareness of the sublime qualities of fairness, generosity, mercy, and grace toward others. Acknowledgment of the priority of these qualities over our basic survival instinct is a significant component of that which distinguishes the human creature from all others. To push them aside is to abandon the grandeur of human "being" and settle for a mere physiological "existence" that falls far short of the potential that lies within all of us.

A second insight worth extrapolating from my experience with the enraged yellow jackets is that of appreciating humor wherever it is found. Once the pain subsided, I could not restrain a smile when I thought of the experience. I must have looked pretty ridiculous as I fled from the yard in panic and slammed through the house looking for relief from the pain. Thoughts of dignity and decorum were the last thing on my mind.

Have you ever reflected upon how much time each of us spends wondering and worrying about what others think about us and our actions? I have come to the conclusion that others observe and think about us much less than we suppose they do. In fact, I suspect my neighbors are so preoccupied with wondering and worrying about what I think about them that they rarely think about me at all.

On occasion, usually in moments of sharp verbal exchange, we remind another, "You are not the center of the universe!" What is ordinarily left unfinished in that sentence is our certainty the other is not the "center of the universe" is predicated upon our equal certainty that we are.

A part of the reason I get a chuckle from remembering my undignified retreat from the yellow jackets is that they "stingingly" reminded me they have a place in the universe as well. Stored carefully in a bank's safe deposit box is a deed declaring that I own the property and house where my wife and I dwell. But the yellow jackets demonstrated clearly that they were in possession, at least of the property, that day.

A third thought emerging from my reflection upon this particular episode is that, while we as persons should avoid decision making based purely upon survival instinct, life still obligates us to sometimes make decision that will cause pain and suffering for others. Late that evening I filled a small bottle with kerosene and, returning to the front yard, located the hole that marked the entrance to the yellow jacket nest. I poured the kerosene down the hole knowing full well that my action would result in the death of the yellow jackets. Why would I do such a thing? Was it a matter of revenge or getting even for the injury they had done to me? Of course not! I destroyed the yellow jacket nest because I have three grandchildren who play in that same space when they come to visit with "Gee-Mommy" and "Gee-Daddy." As surely as real life is never simply "this" or "that," but "this and that inextricably mixed together," real decisions, made in a real world, have real consequences. Sometimes the choice of "this" necessitates the consequence of "that." As a small boy, the father of my grandchildren had severe allergic reactions to stings and bites from ants, hornets, yellow jackets, bees, and such like. His children have inherited this propensity. Thus, the choice to protect them from injury, and possible death, had as its consequence the elimination of the yellow jacket nest.

At this point you may justifiably ask, "What is different about your conscious decision to protect the living space of your grandchildren, and the yellow jackets' unconscious decision to protect theirs? The answer is, "very little." The only justification I can give is the assertion that I value the health and well being of the children more highly than I did the existence of that particular nest of yellow jackets. Decisions must be value based. Otherwise they are simply arbitrary reactions to random stimuli. Thus it is incumbent upon every person to reflect responsibly upon the values that guide one's life. And a genuinely responsible person's value system will encompass, and give due consideration, to both self and others. Further, such a value system, to use the language of the philosophical ethicists, will be both deontological (motive based) and teleological (consequence based). Or put more simply, such a value system will be concerned to do the right thing the right way for the right reasons.

Such reflection upon the value system that guides one's decision making must be done prior to the immediate need to make a decision. Otherwise, in the stress of the immediate circumstances, our actions are more likely to be instinctive reactions than value-based responses. The difference between the two is the difference between saying, "I have done this; now let me think of some reasons to justify my actions." Or saying, "I have reasoned carefully upon the values I hold highest in life, and my action is logically consistent with my value commitments." Such careful reflection upon value commitments will not keep us from still having, from time to time, to make decisions that cause others pain and suffering. But at least the injuries we inflict will not be arbitrary, random, thoughtlessly insensitive, or purely selfish. While it is not humanly possible for us to always do "good" and never do "harm," deliberate thought can, at least, enable us to maximize the "good" and minimize the "harm."

My final observation, emerging from my serio-comic encounter with a nest of annoyed yellow jackets, is the conclusion that the grass does still have to be mowed. By this I mean, decisions must be made and will be made, either actively or passively. The choice to not choose is still a choice, a decision. To do nothing is to do something.

Sometimes, in the midst of real life, if I may paraphrase Shakespeare, "the *stings* and arrows of outrageous fortune" cause us great pain and suffering. The shock may be so great that, at least for a time, we are incapacitated. In a way analogous to the way I fled into the house and soothed the stinging pain with cold water, oral medication, and rest, we retreat into some safe haven to nurse our injuries and renew our spirits. But, inevitably, if we are to be mentally and emotionally healthy, we must return to the activity of living. We must resume the tasks at hand. We must risk the possibility that we will be stung again. Otherwise the

82

weeds of fear and dread will choke out the beauty and vitality of our lives. Certainly we should learn to be more wary of the yellow jackets, but we should return to mow the grass. Why? Because, late in the evening when the breeze rustles through the trees, when the air is filled with the smell of new mown grass, and children laugh and play while the birds flit over- head, it is evident that, on balance, life still has more joy and pleasure in it than it has pain and suffering.

CHAPTER FIFTEEN
God, Don't Take Me Out of the Desert, Just Take the Desert Out of Me

A man can spend two decades of his adult life preparing to do that which he is convinced God has called him to do. He can ask his wife and children to sacrifice the ordinarily expected accouterments of an average, middle-class American lifestyle in order that the man may spend years acquiring the educational credentials to even be seriously considered for a position doing what God has called him to do. Having finally acquired such a position, he can strain with all his might to evoke excellence from others, and challenge them to love and serve God passionately. And then one day he can be called into an office and told by another that his services are no longer required, that his career is over, that his usefulness is at an end. And he can walk out the door and into a desert where alone, unconsoled, suffering at the very core of his being, he calls out to the God whom he has followed all those years, and all he hears in response to his agonized cry is silence.

The Bible contains many thematic images that hold its narrative together. One particularly interesting cluster of images are those associated with geography: Land, Mountain, Water, Wilderness, Garden, River, Desert. In recent years, especially after spending the summer of 1997 in the desert region of Central Jordan, I have been particularly intrigued by the desert/wilderness theme. Within the biblical literature this theme symbolizes many things: isolation and danger, retreat and reflection, refining and preparation, judgment and death.

In Genesis the conversion of Eden's garden into a desert is seen as one of the consequences of human sinfulness. A common theme running through the lives of many of the Bible's central personalities is that

each experiences a solitary sojourn in the desert. In the desert Cain faces
the truth about himself and the enormity of his crime, and throws himself
upon the merciful protection of God. In the wilderness Moses turns aside
from tending his father-in-law's flocks and encounters God in the burning
bush. For forty years the People of Israel wander in the desert while a
faithless generation dies and a new one is prepared to inherit the promise
God made to Abraham, Isaac, and Jacob. In the desert David conceals
himself from the wrath of Saul and refines the skills that will ultimately
make him Israel's greatest king. Elijah, fearing the vengeance of Jezebel,
flees to the safety of the desert and there he hears the still, small voice of
God. From the wilderness John emerges, clad in the garments of the
desert monastic, to announce the presence of God's Anointed. In the
desert Jesus is tempted by the Evil One to betray his purpose for being,
and is ministered to by the angels. Saul of Tarsus retreats to the desert
after witnessing the Resurrected Jesus on the Road to Damascus, and
there he is schooled in the gospel that he fearlessly proclaimed across the
Roman Empire.

In the Bible the desert threatens, it crushes, it consumes, it de-
stroys. But that same desert also pours water from its rocks (Nu. 20:11),
it rejoices (Is. 35:1), it sings (Is. 35:2), it springs forth with rivers (Is.
43:19), and it blossoms like a rose (Is. 35:1). That is the nature of the
desert as geography; it is both negative and positive, it is threatening and
sustaining, it is both merciless and surpassingly beautiful, it is a preview of
hell, and a place to meet and be met by God.

Experience suggests to me that the desert is both a place, and a
state of being. As a place the desert is what it is; positive and negative,
threatening and intriguing. But in the final analysis this desert is only environment; it is external. As a state of being the desert is a choice; it is the
product of one's own volitional will; it is the consequence of how one
copes with the circumstances of life; it is internal. And so, if a man or
woman's constant prayer is, "God, take me out of the desert!" he/she is
likely to hear only silence. But, what are the possibilities if she/he chooses
to change the petition and learns to pray, "God, take the desert out of
me"?

The young woman, recently diagnosed with a terminal illness, wrote
through her tears, "At this point, I'm not really sure prayer works anymore – or even if it's worth the effort. I've tried to be faithful all my life,

but right now I'm not really sure where it has gotten me." Before moving too swiftly to judgment, let me suggest that if you haven't already been where she is, it is highly likely that one day you will be. Despite the biblical truth that genuine grace is unmerited, unearned, and undeserved; our rational being searches for some kind of meritorious balance in our existence. That is why novels, and movies, and TV shows where the "good guys" ultimately triumph over the "bad guys" appeal to us so much. Deeply rooted in human consciousness is the need for some harmonious balance in life. While intellectually we know that "bad things happen to good people" and "good things happen to bad people" such intellectual insight is hardly gratifying and is, in no way, consoling to the battered psyche. Our "gut" still tells us that goodness, integrity, faithfulness, hard work, and compassion for others should count for something in the day to day business of living. When "all things" don't appear to be "working together for good" we want to know why. And pious platitudes suggesting that "everything that happens has a purpose, we just don't know what it is right now," make you want to punch the well-meaning latter-day friends of Job right in the mouth.

And so it is hard, it's very hard, to pray, "God, don't take me out of the desert. Just take the desert out of me." But one still wonders, what might happen if, in the midst of the most devastating of personal circumstances, one learned to pray such a prayer. The following are only suggestions, but to those who are struggling, I hope they will be helpful.

First, such a prayer does not call upon God to repeal the basic laws of physics that hold the universe together in order to solve our personal existential crises. In the poignancy of our personal pain, we often forget that there are others who suffer as profoundly as we do. There is a "thrownness" in the existence of all of us. Thus, questions of "Why me?", "Why now?", "Why here?" are never particularly helpful. It's a lot like saying, "I didn't ask to be born." Tell me, who did? No rational professional person wants to be unemployed. No sane "thirtysomething" wants to die. Such wallowing in the desert is a dead end; common sense, if not faith, calls upon us to move on.

Second, such a prayer reminds us that, ultimately, it is not our circumstances that give shape to the quality of person we are. Rather, our personhood is expressed in how we deal with our circumstances; whatever those circumstances happen to be. Like the desert, our circumstances can threaten, crush, consume, and destroy if we allow them to do so. On the other hand, we can choose to transcend the circumstances; we can choose to rejoice and blossom like the desert rose. I mean more here than the trite assertion, "If life hands you a lemon, make lemonade." I mean that wholeness, character, and authentic personhood emerge from the inside out; they are not imposed from the outside in.

Third, the desert is a fact, a reality, a constant in human experience. As surely as there are mountaintops and oceans, ripening fields and babbling streams, there are deserts. But there is a dynamic quality to our personhood that makes it possible for us to grow, develop, mature, and become. Sometimes circumstances require that we live in the desert, but the desert lives in us only if we allow it to. Like the Gadarene Demoniac of Luke 8, we can, on the edge of the wilderness, inhabit the tombs of what might have been. Or, by God's grace, we can remember who we are, and in the recovery of our identity apart from our circumstances, those who come to see will find us liberated from the demons of doubt, clothed in the garment of rationality, and sitting calmly in the presence of the One who both made us, and Who sustains our being.

Finally, the prayer, "God, don't take me out of the desert. Just take the desert out of me," calls us to distinguish the difference between loneliness and being alone. The desert is a lonely place. But we are alone there only if we choose to be. The stories of Cain, Moses, Elijah, David, John, Jesus, and Paul testify to the desert loneliness, the solitary isolation of each of them. Yet, each knew that he was not ultimately alone, not utterly abandoned; each knew that his voice was heard: "In my distress I called upon the Lord, and cried unto my God: he heard my voice out of his temple, and my cry came before him, even into his ears" (Ps. 18:6 KJV).

And, if we are willing to listen, we will hear the voice of God in the silent stillness of the wilderness. More often than not God's voice will be heard in the voice and presence of another. Moses heard God in the voice of Aaron, his brother, and Zipporah, his faithful wife. David heard God in the presence of Jonathan, the son of his tormentor. Paul heard God speak in the dying words of the martyred Stephen. And that is why, even though life often requires that we live in the desert, we should never allow the desert to live for long within us. For it is not the heat of the desert's day, nor the cold of its night; it is not the desert's arid wastes, rocky precipices, and deadly predators that are the greatest danger to our continued existence. Rather, it is our choice to remain in isolation when, through the presence of others, God offers shade from the heat, warmth from the cold, living water to slake our thirst, and a vigilant shepherd to protect us from the hyena, the lion, the viper, and the precipice.

Somewhere in the heart of every desert there is a place where water, long confined beneath the nearly impenetrable layers of sunburned rock, comes roiling to the surface and spills out onto the sand. Here trees grow and flowers bloom and weary travelers pause to rest and refresh themselves before continuing the journey. It is the oasis, an island of life in the midst of the desert, a shelter and haven from the swirling dust-devil and desiccating heat.

Somewhere in the heart of every lonely soul wandering in the desert of fear, sickness, disappointment, guilt, and isolation there is just such an oasis. There is a verdant, vibrant, core of pulsating life where hope comes bubbling to the surface from beneath the rocky layers of despair and doubt. Perhaps the path that leads through the trackless waste of the desert has its beginning in the oasis that lies at its center. And so, I am learning to pray, "God, help me not be so preoccupied with looking at the desert that surrounds me that I miss the oasis within me. Don't take me out of the desert. Just take the desert out of me."

CHAPTER SIXTEEN
Baptists and Ladybugs

Shortly after moving to Western North Carolina, I became acquainted with the seasonal phenomenon of ladybugs. In the late fall, as the sun takes a more southerly angle in the sky, it shines directly through a large picture window in the west wall of my home study. As the glass and surrounding wall are warmed by the sunlight of late afternoon ladybugs, by the dozens, emerge from every crack and cranny of window and doorsill. It matters little how carefully the joints have been caulked and painted. Somehow, some way, the ladybugs find a way to get inside. They never seem to do much harm, and my cat, Dutch, and I are fascinated by them. For me, their ceaseless movement has the same mesmerizing effect as tropical fish in an aquarium. Unconsciously I begin to watch, and when consciousness returns, I find that several minutes have passed, and I have no recollection of what transpired within them. For Dutch, who is equally fascinated, the interest is decidedly different. To him the ladybugs are, at best, living toys with which to play and, at worst, dietary supplements. He stalks, crouches, pounces, torments, and devours.

Late one afternoon I was passing through the entrance foyer of the sanctuary of the church I was serving at the time. Sunlight streamed through the transom panes over the classic Georgian doors of the main entrance. And, you guessed it, the glass and surrounding woodwork were covered with dozens of ladybugs. And so, taking advantage of a finely crafted Windsor chair in the foyer, I sat down to watch for a while. Each bug, apparently oblivious to the others, traced its own seemingly random pattern across glass and woodwork. Occasionally one would fly in a short arc away from the pane only to land almost immediately a few inches away. Others would disappear and reappear through the cracks in the trim around doors and windows. Yet others sat perfectly still, seemingly asleep or, perhaps, even deceased.

It was one of my days for musing on "things" and so I sat there in the Windsor chair and mused for a while. After a time the thought passed through my mind that ladybugs are a lot like both the best and the worst of Baptists. While the following observations may be true of others within the Christian community, this preacher is deeply rooted within the Baptist tradition. Thus both my critique and my commendation emerge from a sympathetic heart that observes from the inside.

The idea, senseless as it may seem to you, seemed to me worth pursuing for a while so I pursued it. First, there is this seasonality about the ladybugs. While occasionally you see them at other times, for the most part, they are highly visible only in late fall. Some Christians are like this. It appears there is something in their psychological make-up or body chemistry that draws them out in the open only at certain seasons of the year. There are those who are always present for the pageantry and music of the Advent season. Others make their appearance only at Easter. Still others seem to have antennae that detect critical decision-making times. Out of sight most of the time, when a new pastor is to be called, or a critical discussion is being held, or an important vote is to be taken, mysteriously emerging from whatever cracks and crannies they inhabit, these people have their say and vote their conscience. Then, the crisis having passed, they disappear once again into the woodwork, leaving everything but the decision-making to someone else.

One action that apparently makes sense to the ladybug, but makes none to me, is that of flying away only to light and then fly away and light again for no obviously discernible reason. This behavior reminds me of many Baptists I have known. One day they land in a particular congregation, having flown for whatever reasons, from a neighboring church. After a short stay they fly away again and light somewhere else. Flitting from church to church, they never seem able to be satisfied where they are. When asked it's always, "The preacher," or "Those deacons," or "That thing that happened," or some variation of a dozen other complaints. For whatever reasons, they seem to lack the capacity to find lasting satisfaction in any one place. And it never occurs to them to consider that the problem may lie as much within themselves as it does with their external geography or circumstances.

As I mused upon the ladybugs, one of the things I noted was an apparent meaningless, aimless, incessant wandering across the surface of windowpanes and woodwork. While often this wandering has an almost frenetic energy associated with it, it lacks any evident purpose. The ladybugs hurry and scurry but never seem to be going anywhere. Again, I've known Baptists like this. We are a people of incessant activity. There is an old joke about a church that required prospective members to take a physical exam before they were allowed to join. The membership committee wanted to be sure that new parishioners were strong enough to keep pace with all the activities they were expected to attend, participate in, plan, and lead. I actually know of a church that requires members to sign a waiver form absolving the church from responsibility for any injury they may sustain while participating in the church's activities.

Oftentimes Christians have great difficulty discerning the difference between frenetic religious activity and authentically meaningful religious experience. Thus, like the ladybugs, we hurry and scurry, but often seem not to be going anywhere. Perhaps this is one reason for the frequency of "burnout" experienced by both ministers and congregational lay leaders. Activity without purpose is unable to provide the sense of accomplishment all persons need in order to remain healthily motivated and committed. Christian purpose must be rooted in realities that are deeper than competition with neighboring churches, denominational "horse and pony shows," or whatever the mega-churches have declared to be currently fashionable. It is only by being deeply rooted in the redemptive purposes of God that congregations can avoid the roller coaster of institutional bi-polarity where we either engage in obsessive hyper-activity, or plunge into the abyss of apathetic depression.

But that's enough negative. It also occurs to me that there is much about the activity of ladybugs that is both admirable and worth imitating. A close examination reveals that they are covered by a rather tough, and decidedly attractive, outer shell. While the term "Hardshell" Baptist has theological connotations beyond the scope of this reflection, over the years I have come to admire the quality of tough-mindedness that characterizes many of my Christian sisters and brothers. As persons of faith, they are committed for the long haul, and are not easily spooked or dismayed by the strange behavior and muddled thinking that often manifests itself in religious groups. They have heeded the biblical writer's caution that "a double-minded man is unstable in all his ways" (James 1:8). Such persons understand that faith and rationality are not polar opposites, and that the exercise of faith does not require one to check one's brain at the door of the church building. Therefore, undaunted by the criticism they often receive for being too "right-brained," or hard-headed," or "logical," they continually ask questions such as, "Have we considered the long-term consequences of this decision?" or "Is this plan, or program, or action consistent with the purpose of the church as a redemptive community in the world?" They are not obstructionists, and it is unjust to perceive them as such. On the contrary, these are the people who frequently keep us from doing the foolish, and occasionally keep us from doing the disastrous.

Another trait I admire in ladybugs is their ability to navigate through the most narrow cracks and crevices as they make their way through life. I have great admiration for Christians who, undaunted by circumstances and obstacles, determinedly find a way to accomplish what they are convinced God is leading them to do. Often we say, "If it is God's will, He will make a way." There is nothing wrong with this, but sometimes what we leave unsaid is the assumption that God's way is the path of least resistance. Thus, when challenges arise and suffering begins, we conclude rather quickly that God's will must be along another, easier path. We forget that ancient Israel was not delivered from the wilderness, but preserved through it. Perhaps we should add to our assertion "if it is God's will, He will make a way," the further assertion that "if it is God's will, He expects us to find a way."

It may be that the most interesting thing to me about the behavior of ladybugs is that, on closer examination, there does appear to be a purposefulness about their activity. While superficially, much of their behavior seems sporadic, erratic, frenetic, and irrational, there appears to be a single centering constant that never varies. As I watch them regularly on the large plate glass windows of my home study or, on this particular day, as they traversed the small transom panes of the church's entrance foyer, they all seemed instinctively, relentlessly, even passionately, drawn to the sunlight that streamed through the glass.

Jesus said, "I am the light of the world. Whoever follows me will never walk in darkness, but will have the light of life" (Jn. 8:12 NIV).

There is no question that much of our behavior as Christians is as sporadic, erratic, frenetic, and irrational as that of ladybugs. Nevertheless, that which characterizes the true Christian personality is that he/she is inexorably, instinctively, relentlessly, passionately drawn to the S-O-N-light of Jesus Christ that streams through the often dingy glass of human circumstances. It is the light of God's Son that gives meaning and purpose to our existence. This life-giving Light warms and sustains us. And, as we follow the Light, we discover the reason for our existence.

And so, my friend, the next time a Christian sister or brother "bugs" you, before, like my cat, Dutch, you squash and devour them, take the time to observe their behavior. While their words and actions may not always seem sensible, eventually, if you watch them long enough, you may find they are being drawn toward the Son Light of God's love. And, if you follow them, you will "walk in the light as He is in the light" and you will "have fellowship one with another" (I Jn. 1:7 KJV).

One last thought has to do with this business of musing on "things." Periodically all of us need some time for contemplation. We need to allow God to speak to us through the basic senses with which we have been endowed. Too often we are guilty of limiting God to speaking only in religious modes, or in "the language of Zion." We become so "ear" oriented, we are insensitive to various other ways God may reveal Himself to our consciousness. And, in a culture that has become so sensorially desensitized that we fail to perceive much unless it shocks us, God's presence in the mundane and ordinary is too often missed.

A question I frequently ask is, "What have you seen God doing lately?" Often those who hear the question are frustrated because they have attuned themselves only to see the activity of God in the grandly miraculous. If God doesn't hit them between the eyes like a sledgehammer, or blast their ears like a "boom box," or overpower them with ecstatic emotional feelings, then God isn't saying or doing anything. On the other hand, as we learn to reflectively practice the presence of God, we discover that God can speak just as profoundly in the innocuous movement of a ladybug across a windowpane as He does in the overwhelmingly dramatic. The problem is never whether or not God is speaking; that is always a given. The challenge is to discipline and attune our senses so that whether God speaks in the burning bush and fiery chariot, or in the lowly ladybug, He will always find us listening.

CHAPTER SEVENTEEN
There's No Bully Worse Than a Bully for Jesus

It has been over forty years, but I remember him well. Tall, broad-shouldered, a veritable wall of overbearing hostility, and only twelve years old. He was the self-appointed school bully at Wyomina Park Elementary School in Ocala, FL, and I was, he thought, destined to be his next victim. I had all the marks of an easy prey: A new kid at the school, I was small and undernourished. The son of an itinerate construction worker, my voice betrayed that I was from somewhere else, and my clothes were evidence my family was poor. But what was worse, our seating assignments in class were side by side, and when the teacher called on him he sat in defiant silence. When she called on me I usually knew the answer. So new, small, weak looking, and smart; I was just too much to tolerate. I needed to be taught a lesson.

I can close my eyes and see him saunter across the playground, followed by the usual knot of hangers-on who wanted to watch. He taunted; I replied defiantly. (No one ever said I wasn't feisty.) He drew the line; I stepped across it. He swung and I got lucky, for he missed and I didn't. His fist brushed past the side of my head, and mine connected squarely with his nose and upper lip. Suddenly, blood spurted from everywhere, and it was all over. One teacher had me by the arm and another had him. We both ended up in the principal's office, and in those days of corporal punishment, you know what happened next. (I was rather pleased that he felt pain on both ends while I stung on only one.) Afterwards he gave me a wide berth and, a few weeks later, my father moved us on to the next town and the next job. And my brush with the Wyomina Park Elementary bully became just another childhood memory.

Bullies are not an endangered species. Over the decades I have seen, and sometimes had to interact with, other bullies. They come in all shapes and sizes, both male and female. Some are respected members of the community, and others are from the "dregs" of society. Some are well educated and others are illiterate. Some are wealthy; others are poor. Some are profane and others are pious. Some bully with physical violence while others use money, influence, family relationships, religious affirmations, and many other tools to assert their dominance. But bullies, it seems to me, have certain identifying characteristics.

Most bullies I have known seem to be rather insecure in their innermost personhood. The swagger, assertiveness, and intimidation frequently reflect over compensation. Bullies are fearful that others perceive them the way they perceive themselves. This obsessive fear of being found inadequate, or of being laughed at, or of being hurt, is transmuted into a smoldering anger that drives the bully to get his/her "licks" in first. Thus the frightened child on the inside of the bully denies the truth by pretending to be confident, strong, and assertive on the outside.

A second thing I have observed about bullies is their tendency to pick victims they have decided cannot really threaten them. Spousal and child abuse illustrate this point well. The bully is careful to select a victim who appears weaker physically, economically, educationally or otherwise. Bullies prey on persons with low self-esteem and compliant natures. They look for people who are already in, or who can be forced into, subordinate roles in the bully's life. Whether the bully is spouse, parent, neighbor, employer, school mate, political figure, pastor, or whatever, he/she usually picks on someone the bully is sure can be whipped physically, or verbally, or economically, or socially.

Bullies I have known usually have highly fixed opinions, and are uniformly resistant to entertaining alternative points of view. Such bullies, when they ask what you think, really want you to repeat back to them what they think. In addition, bullies have great difficulty sharing the "spot light" with others. A deep-seated sense of personal inadequacy drives them to clutch every vestige of accomplishment and success in a tight-fisted refusal to share.

Akin to the bully's tendency to be over possessive with what is his is the, often conscienceless, willingness to appropriate what belongs to another as his or her own. Finally, the bully has a badly underdeveloped sense of "fair play." She reasons that any conduct is acceptable if it gets the desired results. Thus falsehood, unfair advantage, cheating, theft, manipulation, and threat are simply "tools of the trade" for the bully. The bully says, "I need to build up myself by putting you down; and I'll do whatever is necessary to insure that I come out on top."

The most oppressive bullies I have encountered are religious bullies. There's just no bully worse than a bully for Jesus. In his magnificent novel, *Hawaii*, James A. Mitchner gives us the definitive model of the "bully for Jesus." Abner Hale has just the right combination of neurotic insecurity, priggish self-righteousness, warped ego, and inflexible will to make him one of the least loved characters in modern American literature. Abner bullies his wife, his fellow missionaries, the aboriginal peoples of Hawaii, and almost everyone else who crosses his path. Using the Bible as his mortar, and rigid hyper-Calvinism as his pestle, Abner grinds to dust every personality, every idea, every aspiration, every hope and dream that is not his own. And his only limitation comes in the form of Captain Rafer Hoxworth, who is an even bigger bully than Abner Hale.

Maybe I am oversensitive, but recent decades seem to have witnessed the emergence of increasing numbers of "bullies for Jesus." This phenomenon is probably the consequence of a number of factors in modern culture. I would include among them the increasing de-personalization of society; the decline of authoritative institutions that has been accompanied by an increase in authoritarian voices; the adoption, by the religious community, of a corporate "bottom line" mentality that measures effectiveness solely on the basis of that which is objectively quantifiable; an increasing sense of personal lack of control over one's own future; and the compartmentalization of belief systems and ethical values in such a way that they do not influence and inform one another.

Such an environment is ideally suited to the production of religious bullies; personalities who are determined to control and shape the priorities of the Christian community, local churches, theological education, social concerns, and political issues. By now some of you are saying, "Hold on a minute! Aren't sincere Christians supposed to be concerned about the shape and priorities of the Christian community? Aren't we supposed to be interested in theological education? Don't we have a word to speak in the arena of social concerns? Are we not entitled to a political voice in our society?" The answer to all these questions is, "certainly." Such involvement in modern culture is consistent with the biblical concept of "Christian witness," and we are compelled to such actions by the claims of the "gospel." It is not appropriate religious "zeal" that troubles me; it is an unreflective religious "zealotry" that, in combination with certain traits of personality (both individual and collective), lends itself to fostering the emergence of a "bullying spirit" within the Christian community.

Perhaps you are asking, "Can you give us specific illustrations of this "bullying spirit" that you see manifesting itself in contemporary American Christian religious expression?" Yes indeed. Have you taken note of the increasing frequency with which some use ridicule to undermine the faith assertions of others? Listen to religious broadcasting, read articles and editorials in various religious publications. See how often one "Christian" or "Christian group" makes another "Christian" or "Christian group" the butt of a joke, a caricature, a "straw" opponent. This tactic is as old as human debate. It is the classic Argument *Ad Hominem* (against the person) in which an attack is made upon the person who asserts or defends a particular position, rather than directly engaging the position. It is often easier to attack the person than it is to refute the argument. By use of public ridicule the opponent is "bullied" into submission, or so thoroughly discredited that no one will listen when he seeks to defend himself.

Another example of the emergence of this "bullying spirit" is the increasing frequency with which creedal litmus tests are used to determine the employment future of persons who work for churches, Christian educational institutions, and denominational organizations. The individual or group in the power position says, "Subscribe to my (our) understanding or become unemployed." Certainly a case can be made for the need for doctrinal/theological consensus within any religious institutional structure. But consensus does not require the creation of cloned replicates of an overbearing central personality, or the development of religious automatons who subordinate conscience to security, and parrot the party line in order to keep paying the mortgage. In these instances the threat of becoming unemployed and professionally "black balled" is used to "bully" ministers, faculty members, administrators, denominational workers, missionaries, and others into submission. Vocational workers within the Christian community should not be forced to prostitute themselves in order to remain employed.

Evidence of this kind of "bullying spirit" is not confined to a narrow segment of the contemporary Christian community. It is to be found everywhere along the continuum of fundamentalist, conservative, moderate, and liberal theology. "My way, or the highway," transcends all ideological, denominational, creedal, and political differentiation among Christians. "Bullies for Jesus" are found everywhere.

Observation demonstrates that this "bullying spirit" is not confined to how Christians relate to one another. As, in recent decades, Christians have become more politically active in our culture, some rather disturbing changes have taken place in the way Christian voices express their opinions and convictions. Increasingly, it appears that Christians are becoming comfortable with the use of violence, in one form or another, as a means of exerting "Christian" influence. As Christians have entered the arena of political and social activism, many of the least attractive tactics of partisan politics have become the weapons of choice of the self-appointed defenders of Christian values. Thus, some political figures are "targeted" for "elimination" through the electoral process. Innuendo and character assassination have become acceptable instruments for influencing public opinion. Christians have learned to play "hardball" with political action committees, media events, and massive political war chests. Some few, in the name of Christian values, have even resorted to terrorist bombings and other reprehensible acts in order to further their goals. And sadly, not nearly enough Christian voices have been raised in protest against these criminal actions.

One wonders, "Are not some behaviors unacceptable on the part of those who name the name of Jesus Christ, no matter what the circumstances?" Only a cursory examination of the New Testament is needed to demonstrate that its writers were convinced there must be a consistency between the goals of Christian believers and the means they use to attain them. Thus Paul could say to the Thessalonians, "Make sure that nobody pays back wrong for wrong, but always try to be kind to each other and to everyone else" (I Thes. 5:15 NIV). He admonished the Romans, "Do not be overcome by evil, but overcome evil with good" (Rom. 12:21 NIV), and encouraged them to "not allow what you consider good to be spoken of as evil" (Rom. 14:16 NIV). Certainly the example of Jesus stands as the supreme model of the refusal to resort to violent behavior as a means of advancing the "kingdom of God." The manifestation, and magnification, of a "bullying spirit" as a strategy for human interaction within the Christian community, or as a means of expressing Christian concerns within the secular culture, is counter-productive at best, and essentially un-Christian at worst. From time to time it may be necessary, in the spirit of Christ, to stand up to the bullies of the world. But we must do so without becoming bullies ourselves, for there's no bully worse than a bully for Jesus.

CHAPTER EIGHTEEN
Experiencing God: Connect the Dots, or Assault in the Darkness?

Growing up in West Alabama in the 1950's and 60's, my spiritual consciousness was shaped by stories deeply rooted in the dramatic revivalism that was the legacy of the Second Great Awakening. Burly men burned red by the hot Alabama sun told how God literally struck them down in the field as they walked behind the plow; or shook them awake with a startling vision in the middle of the night. They were "driven to their knees," "snatched from the jaws of hell," "gloriously saved" by the power of God, and some even experienced a "call to preach" in the same moment. Drawing heavily upon the Old Testament, they described their experiences in terms of Jacob wrestling with the angel by the River Jabbok (Gen. 32), or Moses being attacked by YHWH on his way back to Egypt (Ex. 4). Emphasis was placed on their utter helplessness in the face of a radical expression of the absolute sovereignty of God. Their only alternatives were surrender or death. It was all of God and none of them. And the measure of a man's Christian authenticity, particularly that of a minister, was evaluated in terms of the degree of drama in his experience with his Maker.

The 1970's and 80's found me a young minister in a middle-class American self-help culture, influenced by such popular literature as Dale Carnagie's *How to Win Friends and Influence People,* and Norman Vincent Peale's *The Power of Positive Thinking.* Success in life, both materially and spiritually, was couched in terms of faithful adherence to a series of "rules," or "laws," or principles," or "steps" that, if followed properly, would guarantee success whatever the endeavor. Alcoholics were rehabilitated in a series of "steps." AmWay products were distributed according to carefully prescribed principles of marketing. Even the unconverted were witnessed to using "Four Spiritual Laws," or were guided through the principles of "How to Have a Full and Meaningful Life."

While I was preoccupied with surviving puberty, the pendulum had swung from the God-centered emphasis of Calvinistically influenced revivalism, to a human-centered focus that implied that God was the "Self-actualization" waiting at the end of an appropriate journey of "Behavior Modification." Conversion and spiritual growth became less an encounter with the Divine, and more the achievement of a goal. Under the influence of "Possibility Thinking" religious experience became the spiritual equivalent of Monty Hall's "Let's Make a Deal." Preachers encouraged worshippers to "come on down," sign the card, and enroll in the class. Religious literature emerged suggesting that it was only a matter of learning to properly "fill in the blanks," "cross the T's," and "dot the I's." The beginner could start off with a "Survival Kit." After attaining a proper level of proficiency, one could move on up to "MasterLife." The crowning achievement was "Experiencing God." It was implied that such experiences with God could be mechanically induced by faithfully following the program. Knowing and being known by God was simply a matter of "connecting the dots."

Such polarization of perspective is not new to Christian reflection. For as long as sincere, thoughtful men and women have meditated upon their sense of God's presence, they have tended to lean either toward a model of "confrontation from above," or "renovation from below." In the 2nd and 3rd centuries, Montanism, an early apocalypticism, focused upon Divine revelation from above. Morally rigid and evangelistically zealous, the Montanists upbraided the mainstream church for its moral compromise and lack of fervor. By contrast, in the 6th century, Gregory I wrote his *Pastoral Rule* focusing upon the disciplined character and methodological conduct of the Christian personality. Following Gregory's model, various monastic rules and manuals of spiritual development emerged in the Middle Ages. Time does not permit the tracing of these two streams of tradition down across the centuries to the present. But that they are still with us is clearly reflected in such modern spiritual classics as Francis Thompson's *The Hound of Heaven* who relentlessly pursues, and Thomas Merton's vision of spiritual development as the ascent of *The Seven Storey Mountain*.

What is one to make of this radical difference in understanding how people experience the presence of God? Does God alone search out and confront sinful human personalities? Or do women and men have a natural desire for relationship with the Divine that can be deliberately nurtured, cultivated, and caused to blossom? Put another way, "Does God search out and find us, or do we find God at the end of our search?" Alternatively, is it possible that the Divine-Human/ Human-Divine encounter is the consequence of a double search? Are God and human beings both "the lover" and "the beloved"?

At this point I must pause to say I do not categorically reject either the Divine confrontation, or the human search, model for understanding the believer's experience with God. What I do reject is the tendency of some to embrace a stereotype (usually a caricature) of either model, and maintain that it is the only way in which persons experience God. Perhaps the greatest contribution of William James, in his classic study *The Varieties of Religious Experience*, is to raise our consciousness to the truth that there *are* varieties of religious experience. There is no "one size fits all" way in which the presence of God becomes a transforming reality in a person's life. One has only to consult the scripture to find multiple images of how God's presence is mediated in human experience. Yes, Jacob wrestled with the angel beside the Jabbok, and Moses was assaulted in the night; but Elijah encountered God, not in the cataclysmic thunderstorm, but in a "still, small voice." While Saul of Tarsus was struck blind on the road to Damascus, James and John encountered the Christ while quietly mending their nets after a long night of fishing on the Sea of Galilee.

An historical survey of the lives of formative Christian personalities will be similarly revealing. Augustine of Hippo encountered God at the end of a long intellectual quest. Martin Luther's journey began in a violent thunderstorm where his friend was killed by lightning, and young Martin cried out, "St. Anne, help me, and I will become a monk." John Wesley relates both his fear of Divine judgment on a storm tossed sea, and his sense of being "strangely warmed" while listening to the reading of the preface to Luther's *Commentary on Romans*. There is no need to continue multiplying illustrations. The point is sufficiently made. What is important is that one know and be known by God. For some such intimacy is the product of dramatic confrontation in the midst of crisis; for others it is a calm assurance that creeps across one's consciousness enveloping the recipient in loving belongingness. For one all the pieces come together and she says, "Aha, I get it now!" Another witnesses that from childhood he thinks he has always understood; that there has never been a time when God's loving presence was not a meaningful reality in his life.

If it is agreed that persons appear to experience the presence of God along a continuum bounded on one extreme by stories of sudden, dramatic Divine confrontation, and on the other by stories of deliberate, reflective spiritual discipline; are there any conclusions that may be drawn from this wide range of God consciousness? I think the following are worth considering.

First, such diversity of experience serves as a reminder of the personal character of one's relationship with God. While biblical religion is not a private revelation, it is an intensely personal relationship. The Bible knows nothing of isolated, "Lone Ranger," "You and me alone, God" religion. In the Old Testament, God is revealed as the God of Abraham, Isaac, and Jacob. In the New Testament Jesus' frequent use of the intensely familiar term *Abba* (Father, literally Daddy) speaks eloquently of the depth of His own personal relationship to God. That Jesus taught His disciples to pray "Our Father" indicates that this personal intimacy with God encompassed them, and you and me, as well.

When two persons experience one another, they both bring something to the encounter. Each relationship is given shape and uniqueness as the personhood of one responds to that of the other. It is no surprise that I experience the people around me somewhat differently than another may experience those same people. I assess their openness, warmth, integrity, and value through the lens of the person I am. I have no expectation that everyone will experience my neighbor, my friend, my employer, and certainly not my spouse, in the same way I do.

Why is it then that some seem to have a compulsive need for everyone else's experience of God to be shaped identically to their own? If our experience of others is somewhat "person specific" why should our experience of God not be as well? Some will recoil in horror at this suggestion, and argue that I am simply trying to shape God in my own image, or permit God only those characteristics and qualities that appeal most to me. I will respond that I am doing nothing of the sort.

When Christians speak of God in terms of classical biblical religion, certain defining qualities are absolutely essential. To ignore or eliminate those qualities is to cease to speak of the God of the Bible. Similarly, most persons share a mental picture of the ideal qualities of human personhood. Thus I may experience my neighbor as dishonest, vindictive, selfish, and hateful. However, if others whose opinion and judgment I respect, experience him as honest, gracious, giving, and loving, I am given reason to examine and reconsider the accuracy of my perception. I may be wrong. I may be choosing deliberately to malign the character of my neighbor even when I know better. I may have jumped to a hasty conclusion without adequate experience with my neighbor. Whatever the case, my point is that there are ways for me to test the validity and authenticity of my experience with my neighbor.

It is equally true that there are ways for me to protect against excessive subjectivity in my understanding of, and experience with, God. Is my experience consistent with the understanding of God outlined in classical biblical theology? Is my experience similar to that of others whose opinion and judgment I respect? While I insist that any personal experience need not be exactly like that of another, I also maintain that it cannot be so radically different that it suggests we have not experienced the same God. Thus it may be asserted that the "person specific" quality of one's encounter with God has an appropriate place within the context of understanding that "personal" and "private" do not mean the same thing. A Christian's personal religious experiences must be tested against the "public" nature of biblical religion. While, from the biblical perspective, there is no authentic knowledge of God apart from *covenant* in the Old Testament and *ecclesia/koinonia* in the New Testament, the "person specific" quality of Divine encounter is maintained. While the individual is included in the collective *covenant* or *ecclesia/koinonia*, he/she is not absorbed and obliterated in it.

A second conclusion has to do with the nature of Divine revelation. The scripture witnesses to the fact that God elects to accommodate the Divine self-disclosure in relation to our capacity to grasp and understand. Thus God says to Moses at Sinai, "I appeared to Abraham, to Isaac and to Jacob as *El Shaddai* (God Almighty), but by my name *YHWH* (I Am) I did not make myself known to them" (Ex. 6:3 NIV). Similarly, in the New Testament, the disciples of Jesus often understood things that were beyond the grasp of the scribes, pharisees, and saducees. "Blessed are you, Simon, son of Jonah; for flesh and blood has not revealed this unto you, but my Father who is in heaven" (Mt. 16:17 KJV). On the other hand, sometimes even His nearest followers were not prepared to understand what Jesus told them (see Jn. 11:11-14). Such statements are not a license to claim a type of *Gnostic* private revelation that sets one apart from, and above, other believers. Rather, they are the acknowledgment that different persons are at different places in their pilgrimages of spiritual development, and that God, in fact, meets us where we are, as we are. From there He moves us toward where He ultimately intends for us to be. It is a process that is not complete until we finally live in God's unmediated presence in glory.

Lastly, earlier I raised the question, "Is it possible that the Divine-Human / Human-Divine encounter is the consequence of a double search?" In the relationship with God, as surely as in all other personal relationships, there is, in fact, a reciprocity that is experienced. The great Jewish theologian, Martin Buber, explored this profound reality in his treatise, *I and Thou*. Authentic personal relationships involve both knowing and being known. The ancient psalmist sang, "As the hart panteth after the water brooks, so panteth my soul after thee, O God" (Ps. 42:1 KJV). Likewise, we are told that it was God who came searching for the man and the woman in Eden and called out, "Where are you?" (Gen. 3:8-9). Often I summarize Augustine of Hippo's spiritual pilgrimage, related in his *Confessions*, in the sentence, "Lord, I searched for You, and I searched for You, and I searched for You; and one day You found me."

So, "Experiencing God: Connect the Dots, or Assault in the Darkness?" I would affirm that, if we avoid the caricatures of extremism, it is some of both, and may be characterized by a greater degree of one or the other, depending upon the circumstances and needs of the individual who encounters God. While not a private experience, knowing and being known by God is profoundly personal. If the shape of one's personhood is such that God must speak by Divine confrontation, another, whose personhood is shaped differently, should be willing to respect and affirm the legitimacy of the one who has met God in dramatic confrontation. On the other hand, the experience of those who have met God in quiet meditation and disciplined study and reflection, including the use of some biblically-based literature designed to foster openness to God's presence, should be valued and respected as well. We must remember that what is of primary importance is to know, and to be known by God. The "person specific" details of one's experience are secondary. While the specific details of another's experience may be, positively or negatively, instructive for me, they are not, and should never be considered to be, normative for all who encounter and are transformed by the presence of God. As Christians, we are called to Christ-likeness. That does not necessitate that we become stereotyped clones of one another.

CHAPTER NINETEEN

Spindale Drugstore:
What It Provides That Sometimes the Church Doesn't

About a decade ago I was invited to become interim pastor to a fine congregation in Spindale, NC. What I thought would be a brief interim lasted more than one and a half years, and in that time I developed many meaningful relationships with the people of the Spencer Baptist Church. Not long after arriving in this small community in the North Carolina foothills, I was introduced to one of the town's oldest and most popular institutions. My first visit to Spindale Drugstore was like stepping back into my 1950's and 1960's childhood. Located on a corner of Main Street adjacent to the community center, post office, and public library, Spindale Drugstore is housed in a Depression Era structure complete with high plaster ceiling, whirling ceiling fans, locally constructed display shelves, and much of the ambiance of the corner drugstore of an earlier generation. Founded by a family who has lived in the community for generations, Spindale Drugstore has even maintained the coffee/soda/sandwich shop that was the ubiquitous feature of small town drugstores in mid-20th century America.

On any given day one can stop by the drugstore in the hours between 11:00 A.M. and 1:00 P.M. and watch a substantial portion of the Spindale community as it passes through for lunch. Tables and counter-stools will all be occupied while other patrons wait cheerfully for their turn. The fare is pretty simple and straight forward: sandwiches, potato salad, cole slaw, hot soups, salads, chips, and locally made pies and cakes. My personal favorite is a grilled pimento cheese and bacon sandwich, potato salad (during the winter I substitute hot soup), and coffee. My only complaint is that they routinely serve sweet pickle slices with their sandwiches; I prefer dill.

A very busy schedule does not permit me to do so now, but in years past I occasionally dropped by in the afternoon with notepad and pen in hand, after the lunch crowd had all cleared out. Claiming a booth at the back, I drank coffee served by a pert middle-aged waitress who thought it was "neat" that I was a writer. On more than one occasion I have reflected, from the perspective of one who is deeply involved in the Christian religious community, upon the phenomenon of Spindale Drugstore. I am convinced that one reason for its success is that it consistently provides for its patrons many of the things they should also, but unfortunately do not always, find in the local church.

When one enters Spindale Drugstore, even the casual observer will note the complete absence of social classes and social stratification. Blue collar, white collar, male, female, old and young vie amiably for places to sit during the lunch hour. Warm greetings are exchanged between plumber and insurance agent, educational administrator and shopkeeper, community college professor and textile worker. Tables are shared between middle class retirees out for a casual lunch and artisans and laborers who need to eat quickly and get back to the job. It is a place where business suit and coveralls sit side by side, and each is served with the same promptness, consideration, and amiability as the other.

This community drugstore is also a place where the newcomer is readily accepted and quickly integrated into the culture. One has only to visit two or three times to become a regular. Faces light up with recognition when you enter, and one can always expect a wave, or a nod, or some spoken word of welcome. If you're away for a while, you can count on the waitress, or the cash register operator to ask where you've been and say you were missed. Without being intrusive, folks are inquisitive enough to be sure that everything is O.K., and that you weren't away because of some serious problem. If there has been a serious problem, there is always a sympathetic ear to listen for a moment and commiserate.

Because everyone more or less knows everyone else, Spindale Drugstore is a great place to exchange information and catch up on the latest happenings in the community. While, obviously, some of it is run-of-the-mill, casual gossip; one can also gauge the tenor of public opinion from the weightiest national issues to the smallest of local concerns by listening to the exchanges over lunch. Weddings and childbirths are celebrated, deaths are mourned, illnesses are discussed, and domestic crises aired. In less than an hour, one can hear the competence of local physicians debated, find out about a change in mortgage interest rates at the local bank, hear the proceedings of the town council meeting the night before, and listen to commentary on the quality of last Sunday's sermon at the nearby Baptist, or Methodist, or Brethren, or Presbyterian church.

One of the chief features of the restaurant in Spindale Drugstore is that it provides simple, consistently good food for its patrons served by competent, friendly people. The place and its employees are clean, the basic menu items are fresh, well prepared, and consistent in quality. It makes no pretense at being a gourmet or ethnic restaurant, steak house, fish camp, or purveyor of fast food. They don't do breakfast and they don't do dinner. They do lunch, simple unpretentious, appetite-satisfying lunch, and they do it well. It is evident that the people who run the place understand the needs of their clientele, and the bill-of-fare is a clear response to the needs of the community, not an expression of the personal preferences of the owners and employees.

Akin to the above observations is my sense that institutionally Spindale Drugstore has a clear understanding of its mission in relation to the other primary institutional structures of the community. It is not the banks, or the churches, or the school system, or the civil government, or the business community, or the hospital. It is a locally owned and operated drugstore that fills prescriptions, sells over-the-counter items, and serves lunch in an adjacent soda/coffee/sandwich shop. It doesn't deliver everything, but it does faithfully deliver what it promises to its constituency.

Finally, when I go into Spindale Drugstore, I have a sense that this establishment really belongs to its patrons. It is theirs, not in that they hold title to the property and are proprietors of the business. It is theirs in that it meets a need in their lives, helps them to define themselves as persons, facilitates their meaningful interaction with one another, and provides them with a sense of identity within the larger community. It is theirs, not as a personal possession, but rather as a collective, symbiotic fellowship of giving and receiving. In the best sense of the classical term, it is a *koinonia*, a free association of persons for the mutual benefit of all concerned.

As one who has spent an adult lifetime serving within the contemporary Christian community, I must acknowledge that I do not always find, in the local church, the characteristics discussed above with the same consistency and quality that I find them at the Spindale Drugstore. And yet almost everyone would agree that these characteristics (i.e., acceptance without social distinctions, a sense of being personally cared for, mutual affirmation and burden bearing, basic nurturing, and inclusive ownership) are consistent with the biblical model of what should be reflected within any Christian community of faith.

Why this is true is more the subject of a major book than of a brief reflection such as this. But I would offer a single suggestion that perhaps gets at the crux of the local church's frequent failure to effectively meet the needs of its constituency. Earlier I said, "institutionally Spindale Drugstore has a clear understanding of its mission." Its mission is to serve the community by responsibly dispensing prescription and non-prescription medications and providing a good, economical lunch for people on the move in the heart of the community. That's what it is, and that's what it does; purpose and performance are consistent with one another. Local churches often, it seems to me, fail to minister effectively primarily because of lack of clarity in understanding and commitment to the purpose of the church as described in the New Testament, and most clearly exemplified in the life and ministry of Jesus of Nazareth. Because many local churches fail to understand their purpose, their performance often falls short of what is wished, or intended, or desired, or needed.

An appropriate understanding of purpose involves actively asking and honestly answering two questions in the proper order. The first question is, "What are we?" The second is, "What should we do because of what we are?" Failure in this process is reflected in the plight of many, many local congregations today. Characterized by frenetic activity, confused by conflicting priorities, castigated by a secular culture that views them as harmless and irrelevant at best, and counter-productive and obsolete at worst; churches struggle with declining attendance, internal strife, and loss of moral influence in the wider community. The ancient Hebrew sage was correct when he observed, "Where there is no vision, the people perish . . ." (Prov. 29:18). The word "vision" here could be translated "clearly defined sense of purpose."

Why is sense of purpose so important for any effective institution, particularly a local church? This question has a number of answers. First, clearly defined purpose enables the contemporary Christian community to maintain a sense of continuity with previous generations of believers all the way back to the New Testament era. Continuity with the past is not the same as living in the past. While my nostalgia for childhood in an earlier, simpler time may be triggered by the visual stimuli found in the Spindale Drugstore, I have no desire to return to the mid-20th century and live in that period once again. However, because the decades of the 50's and 60's were my formative years, they significantly contributed to the definition of the person I am. While it is a mistake to attempt to go back to one's sources, it is an even greater mistake to forget one's sources, or attempt to live as though one had no sources. Why I am and who I am are defined, in part, by who I was, and from whence I came. Isaiah challenged the people of his day with the words, "ye that seek the Lord: look to the rock whence ye are hewn . . ." (Is. 51:1).

Second, the church with a clearly defined sense of purpose is comfortable enough with itself that others can be comfortable within it. It is discomfort with one's sense of identity that leads to posturing, pretense, and affectation. Spindale Drugstore does not attempt to be the church, or the bank, or the town hall, or the hospital, or a gourmet restaurant. And the local church should not attempt to be the country club, or the community center, or the political party headquarters, or the police department. People who cannot be comfortable with, and accept themselves, cannot make others feel comfortable and accepted in their midst. But in a place where everyone feels free to come and go, everyone will come and go with regularity. In such a place blue collar, white collar, male, female, old and young can worship together in harmony. Plumber and insurance agent can serve communion; educational administrator and shopkeeper can stand shoulder to shoulder and feed the hungry or care for the dying; community college professor and textile worker can kneel together to pray and rise up together to serve.

Lastly, a commonly held sense of purpose contributes to the achievement of a sense of investment and ownership on the part of a church's members. Now I know that, in the best biblical sense, church members do not own the local church any more than the customers of the Spindale Drugstore own that business establishment. The church, both universal and particular, is owned by the God who called it into being; and who sustains its existence through the redemptive work of Jesus Christ.

Again, I am not talking about who holds the title; I am talking about who participates faithfully and enthusiastically in the collective, symbiotic fellowship of giving and receiving. The church that knows and lives its purpose meets needs in the lives of people; it helps them to define themselves as persons; it facilitates their meaningful interaction with others; and it provides them with a sense of identity within the larger community. It does so because, under God, the local church is a *koinonia*, a free association of persons for the mutual benefit, both here and hereafter, of all concerned.

CHAPTER TWENTY
There Are More Four-Leafed Clovers
Than Most of Us Ever See

In the early 1990's I was afforded the opportunity to serve as interim pastor of a congregation in Gastonia, NC. One warm spring Sunday morning, one of the elderly women and I somehow got into a conversation about four-leafed clovers. I observed that, over a lifetime that had spanned more than four decades, I had never actually found one. She responded, "Why, I see them all the time." With these words, as I watched in incredulous amusement, she hitched up her skirts the way farm women have for centuries, squatted on the sidewalk, and began to point with a bony finger. "There's one," she said. "There's another." And "there's another." In the space of two minutes she pointed out half a dozen four-leafed clovers in an area of no more than nine square feet.

Laughing at my astonishment, she stood up, smoothed out her dress, and headed for Sunday School. The next Sunday she brought me a small collection of four-leafed clovers laminated between two thin sheets of plastic. "These are for a man who can't see to find his own," she said with blunt directness and went on her way. Now, more than ten years later, that collection of clover leafs rests on a bookcase shelf in my personal study. I never see it without fondly remembering the wonderful old woman with the gift of seeing with clarity things that, try as I might, I could never see until they were pointed out to me.

Each summer a grandson, who wasn't even born when I was at the church in Gastonia, comes to spend a week with his grandmother and me. One recent evening I sat on the porch sipping coffee and watching the sunset while Peggy and Jamison watered the flowers beside the walk.

Soon both woman and child were on their knees, and I realized they were searching for four-leafed clovers. A moment later a squeal of delight erupted from the seven year old boy as his grandmother plucked one of these treasures from the ground. Minutes later they found another. In the space of half an hour they found five, and I began to think, "Maybe the world has more four-leafed clovers in it than most of us think."

Is it possible that the perception of the rarity of four-leafed clovers is no more than a myth handed down from generation to generation by people like myself who simply lacked, or failed to cultivate, the perception to see them? Perhaps I don't see four-leafed clovers very often because I have been conditioned to believe they are so rare that it is hardly worth taking time and energy to look for them. If this is true, and I have begun to suspect it may be, how many other things do I miss seeing because I have been conditioned not to look for them?

Maybe I don't see as much goodness in others as I ought because poor biblical interpretation has conditioned me to believe that people are, by nature, bad, rather than good. Perhaps I don't see solutions to problems because I have been conditioned to believe such things are too difficult for me to grasp. Could it be true that I don't see flaws in my own character and judgment because I refuse to see that I am not taking all relevant data into consideration?

When I was a child, my father would often send me on an errand to bring him some tool, or piece of equipment, he needed as he worked at some shade tree mechanic project. Sometimes, in spite of my best efforts, I would fail to see and retrieve what later he would exasperatedly point out was lying right there in the open. As I shuffled my feet in embarrassed humiliation, he would say, "Boy, you can't see for looking." Jesus confronted the spiritually unperceptive of his day with the question, "Having eyes, do you not see?" Such reflection forces me to consider the possibility that my lack of ability to see four-leafed clovers, and many much more important realities, has at least as much to do with "how I look" as it does with the rarity of four-leafed clovers.

What might be the cause of my failure to see what is so obvious to others? Careful thought suggests there may be several factors that need taking into account. First, I wonder if preoccupation with my own dignity is sometimes an obstacle to clarity of vision? Neither the old woman who hitched her skirts and squatted on the sidewalk, nor the grandmother and child crawling on hands and knees in the yard, appeared particularly concerned about the perception others might have of their actions. The old woman in Gastonia found delight in showing her pastoral Ph.D. there are realms of knowing beyond those achieved by poring over moldy library tomes. And the other two simply delighted in frolicking together in the gathering dusk of a sultry summer evening. None of this trio of four-leafed clover finders was so self-absorbed they could not simply relax and enjoy the moment. Sometimes we are so self-conscious we find it impossible to be conscious of anything but self.

Second, is it possible that sometimes I wear perceptive filters that screen out the very things for which I am looking? A number of years ago I participated in an archaeological project in central Jordan. I was part of a team tasked with visiting, assessing the condition of, photographing, and locating by GPS technology, hundreds of archaeological sites on the Kerak Plateau, or the region that was Old Testament Moab. Our instructions were to collect pottery sherds from each place we visited because of the usefulness of pottery in developing the chronology of the occupation of a site. On the first three days we walked site after site and, while my companions picked up literally hundreds of broken pieces of pottery, I found only a few. Finally, I figured out the problem. The blue-blocker, wrap-around sun glasses I wore to protect my eyes from the desert glare filtered out the spectral range necessary for seeing the sherds on the desert floor. I was looking just as carefully as my colleagues, but the sun glasses were filtering out what I needed to see.

We all look at life through filters. Some are called race, others economics, still others philosophical and religious presuppositions, and so forth. If we insist upon wearing these social/cultural filters when it is inappropriate to do so, they make it exceedingly difficult, and sometimes impossible, to discern what is obvious to others. Did I need to protect my eyes from the glare of the desert sun? Certainly! Did I also need to understand that the sun glasses would influence what I saw, or in this case, did not see? Equally certainly! If I really wanted to assist in finding the pottery sherds, did I need to remove, adjust, or change the lenses through which I was looking? Absolutely!

This is equally true of the most important insights of life. If the cultural, psychological, economic, religious, and ethnic filters through which we look obscure or distort our vision, we must be extremely careful how we interpret the information we receive through them. With the best of intentions we may fail to perceive clearly and, thus, act in ways that are detrimental to ourselves and others because we insist on looking at reality through inadequate, or inappropriate, filters.

Third, I wonder if one reason I fail to see four-leafed clovers as readily as others is that, in the midst of the busyness of life, I have lost the sense of joy and delight that accompanies spontaneous discovery. Decades of my life were devoted to the academic pursuits that make it possible for me to put the initials A.S., B.A., M.A., M.Div., and Ph.D. behind my name on business cards and stationery. Over those decades I have become quite adept at the art of taking on large, demanding projects, breaking them down into smaller units, and then mastering each unit or task, one by one, until the whole project has been completed, or the goal achieved. But a price has been paid for the refinement of such disciplined analytic skills. Part of that price has been the loss of some ability to take delight in the simple, ordinary, uncomplicated, sometimes frivolous, joys of life. Maybe there was some truth in my father's often repeated assertion, "Son, you can't see for looking." It is just possible that many important things in life are missed by concentrating too much, being too deliberate, working too hard.

Have you ever mislaid your car keys, or wallet, or purse, and turned the house inside out searching for them, only to discover they were laying right out in the open? When this happens to me, I have the sense it wasn't so much that I found the lost item, as it was that the lost item found me. Maybe that's how it is with four-leafed clovers; maybe we don't find them, but they find us. And maybe those who see them frequently are the people who have cultivated, not the art of finding, but the art of allowing one's self to be found.

Increasingly, I'm intrigued by the notion that life's most important spiritual insights derive more from being found than from finding. They are the product, not of understanding, but of "standing under." It's not so much that we get them, as it is that "they get us." These spiritual insights do not await us at the end of our quests; rather they reveal themselves in times and places when we are not even searching. We do not find them; they find us.

Therefore, I don't think very many four-leafed clovers are found by people who work at finding them. I think they are found by the people

116

who are so open to possibility they can experience the clover's joyous announcement, "Here I am!" And I don't think God is found by the people who work at finding Him. Rather, God finds us, and speaks in the "still, small voice" that announces, "Here I am." God finds us, and allows the heavens to declare His glory. God finds us, and pitches His tent in our midst. God finds us in the midst of the stresses of life, and we are suddenly aware that we are not alone after all.

One last question continues to intrigue me. Are there adjustments I can make in the way I look at life that would assist me in more readily recognizing the presence of God? Surely there are. I think, for the most part, the people who frequently see four-leafed clovers are people who expect to see them. And I think, for the most part, those who witness the activity of God in the world are people who expect to see evidences of God's presence. And so, I have decided to assume a posture of expectancy, trusting that such a posture will enhance my ability to recognize God's presence in the things that are happening before my eyes. This posture of expectancy consists of three resolutions I have made.

First, I have resolved to be more open to the joyous possibility that God prefers relating to me as loving Presence, rather than as righteous Judge. The scripture says, "God is love; and he that dwelleth in love dwelleth in God, and God in him" (I Jn. 4:16). Instead of living in fear that God is going to "get me" if I don't touch all the bases, and dot all the I's, and cross all the T's, I'm going to embrace the belief that God has already "got me" enveloped in the arms of His loving presence. To dwell in the presence of God is to dwell in love.

Second, I have resolved to rest in what God has done, and continues to do for me, in and through the free gift of grace made known in Jesus Christ. While much is achieved through human striving, I have a sense that the most important things are the consequence of trusting acceptance. Again, the scripture says, "For by grace are you saved through faith; and that not of yourselves: it is the gift of God" (Eph. 2:8). In the very next breath the author of Ephesians says, "we are . . . created in Christ Jesus unto good works . . ." (Eph. 2:10). It is not through my human striving that I experience God's grace. Rather, it is through trusting acceptance of God's grace that my human striving is given meaning. As a Christian, I am called to live in a particular way, not in order that I might be saved, but as the consequence of the fact that I have been saved.

Finally, I have resolved to more consciously cultivate an attitude of gratitude for the myriad small wonders of life that are, like the four-leafed clovers, always there, even when we are not specifically aware of them. It is true that there are more four-leafed clovers that most of us ever see. And it is also true that all of us are blessed in countless ways we hardly perceive. This is the wonderful reality discovered by Francis of Assisi, and reflected in his prayer, *The Song of Brother Sun:*

Most High Almighty Good Lord,
Yours are the praises, the glory, the honor, and all blessings!
To You alone, Most High, do they belong,
And no man is worthy to mention You.

Be praised, my Lord, with all Your creatures,
Especially Sir Brother Sun,
By whom You give us the light of day!
And he is beautiful and radiant with great splendor.
Of You, Most High, he is a symbol!

Be praised, my Lord, for Sister Moon and the Stars!
In the sky You formed them bright and lovely and fair.
Be praised, my Lord, for Brother Wind
And for the Air and cloudy and clear and all Weather,
By which You give sustenance to Your creatures!

Be praised, my Lord, for Sister Water,
Who is very useful and humble and lovely and chaste!

Be Praised, my Lord, for Brother Fire,
By whom You give us light at night,
And he is beautiful and merry and mighty and strong!

Be praised, my Lord, for our Sister Mother Earth,
Who sustains and governs us,
And produces fruits with colorful flowers and leaves!

Be praised, my Lord, for those who forgive for love of You

And endure infirmities and tribulations.
Blessed are those who shall endure them in peace,
For by You, Most High, they will be crowned!

Praise and bless my Lord and thank Him
And serve Him with great humility. Amen.
(Frances of Assisi, *The Little Flowers of St. Francis*, tr. Raphael
Brown, Doubleday, 1958, p. 317).

CHAPTER TWENTY-ONE
Why Some Survive the Storms, and Others Don't

Recently I visited Panama City Beach, Florida; one of the places on the Florida Gulf Coast that sustained significant damage when hurricanes Frances and Ivan made landfall there. One day, on a leisurely stroll along the beach, picking my way carefully through the debris left behind by the storm surge, I stood beneath a long concrete fishing pier that reaches out at least a quarter of a mile into the surf. While looking at the relatively undamaged Panama City landmark, I noted certain construction features that suggest why this fishing pier weathered the most recent, as well as previous, storms relatively unscathed while similar structures succumbed to the battering abuse of wind and wave.

One feature, admittedly, has more to do with happenstance than engineering. This particular pier juts out directly southward and, thus, was oriented to meet the storm's surge head on. Like ships that turn their bows into the waves to present their narrowest profile to the swells, this pier was oriented in the best direction at the time of crisis. To some degree this was pure luck. If either hurricane had approached from a more easterly direction, the pier's fate might have been very different had not other matters been attended to by its designers and builders.

It was a second feature of the fishing pier that made possible the structure's survival. The pier is supported by dozens of steel reinforced concrete pillars anchored firmly within the bedrock limestone deep below the sugar white sands of the beach. Staring at the concrete pillars, I caught a glimpse into the secrets of this pier's ability to stand firm through the raging storms. These same secrets explain why, in the midst of the storms of life, some people are ravaged and wrecked while others, though often battered and scarred, weather life's surging tides and tempestuous winds to stand firm as monuments of hope and confident faith.

One secret has already been alluded to; the fishing pier's pillars reach through the sand into the underlying bedrock. Were they only buried in the sand, or even simply resting atop the bedrock, the pier could not have sustained itself against gusting wind and crashing wave. One is reminded of Jesus' story of the man who hurriedly built his house upon the sand, and his neighbor who took the time to dig deeply and root his foundation in the bedrock beneath the soil. When the rains came and the winds blew, one house was reduced to ruins while the other remained a safe, enduring haven for its occupant.

Life frequently tempts us toward shortcuts and superficiality. Impatient for appearance, we build our lives on things and in places that shift under the stress. In our eagerness for instant gratification, we often do only enough to get by, and when the crises come the shaky edifices of our lives cannot withstand the pressure of life's tempests. Life's hardships surge around us washing away the shallow sands and undercutting our hastily erected foundations. Disease, failure, financial collapse, broken relationships, and personal betrayals sweep the supports from beneath us, and we collapse in catastrophic ruin.

Many elect to anchor their lives in material wealth, physical beauty, intellectual accomplishment, athletic ability, talents and gifts, family ties, and dozens of other factors that, while not unimportant, are insufficient to meet the need. Like sand they shift and wash in the surge of changing circumstances. Markets fail, beauty fades, athletes suffer from injury and age, performing talents give way to faltering voices and arthritic joints. These things just do not endure.

What does? Only the reality of God, the One who caused us to be, and Who sustains our being. Only this One whom Paul Tillich described as the "Ground of Being," is a sufficient reality upon whom to anchor our lives. Repeatedly the biblical writers use the rock metaphor to describe God's unchanging constancy in a world where nothing else is ultimately dependable. Just as the columns of the pier are rooted deeply into the limestone bedrock, our lives must be anchored deep within the One the Psalmist describes as "the rock of our salvation" (Ps. 95:1).

A second secret contributing to the endurance of the pier at Panama City Beach is found by examining the materials from which it is made.

Concrete is a remarkable building material resulting from the combination of other substances, in the right proportion, made use of at the right time. Concrete is made from combining sand, gravel or crushed stone, cement, and water in correct proportion. Cement is a binding agent that is the product of mixing burned limestone and clay. When looked at separately these are all pretty ordinary materials. No single ingredient is pre-eminent; it is their dynamic interaction with one another, their chemical bonding, that results in a remarkably durable substance it would be difficult to imagine living without in the modern world.

The analogy to human personhood is not difficult to make. As surely as the concrete consists of both the enduring qualities of the bedrock limestone; it contains the transient plasticity of the sand and clay. As human beings we reflect both the divine qualities of the God who made us, and those of the earth from which we are made. We are neither "this" nor "that." We are "this and that" bound together in dynamic unity.

Proportionality is the key to sustaining ourselves in the midst of life's storms. Excessive emphasis upon our God-likeness leads to the *hubris* (pride) of self-idolatry. Over emphasis upon our identity with the matter of the universe leads to pre-occupation with material, sensual gratification. Too much sand, too much water, too much stone, or too much cement results in concrete that will not stand the stress and strain of wear and exposure over time. The vibrations of traffic, buffeting waves, and blowing wind cause tiny fissures that widen, in time, into deep cracks, that finally lead to failure and collapse. Such is often the story of our lives. Too much of this, or not enough of that, contribute to lives that externally appear sound and strong. But when the vibrating storms come, internal fissures work their way to the surface where they become cracks. The cracks widen as life's storms beat vehemently and finally we fall.

One further thought needs exploring before we move on. When the sand, rock, cement, and water are mixed in the right proportion to form concrete, there is a finite window of opportunity in which the concrete must be used or it becomes useless. If not poured in a timely fashion, concrete will congeal into whatever shape random circumstances impose upon it. When this is allowed to happen pliable potentiality hardens into inflexible fixedness as what could have been freezes into what is.

This leads to a third secret of the fishing pier's ability to endure despite the buffeting hurricanes. Concrete has no value as an amorphous, semi-solid, shapeless mass; something must give it shape. If merely shaped by external circumstance it ends in waste, allowed to run out on the ground it is useless. But, if shaped by deliberate plan and purpose, concrete is one of the most versatile, most useful, substances on the planet.

I looked closely at the pillars supporting the pier, and reflected on two essential shaping realities, one I could perceive with my eyes; the other I knew was hidden below the surface of each concrete column. The passage of time had not worn away the surface marks left on the pillars by the forms unknown workmen erected long before the semi-solid mixture came streaming from trucks specially designed to transport cement mix. It was these carefully constructed forms that kept the concrete, when poured, from running out on the sand and assuming whatever shape random circumstance dictated. Long before they were poured a master engineer devised a comprehensive plan of which each pillar would be a part. The pillars didn't "form" themselves; they were formed in the mind of the master engineer whose plan was executed by workmen who assembled the forms, mixed the concrete, and supervised the pour. God said to Jeremiah:

> *Before I formed thee in the body I knew thee:*
> *And before thou camest forth out of the womb*
> *I sanctified thee* . . . . (Jer. 1:5)

It is not just Adam; God has formed us all from the dust of the earth and breathed the breath of life into us. God's marks upon us (image and likeness) are visible to the discerning eye. Christians describe these marks as Christ-likeness.

But I spoke of two shaping realities in the supporting columns of the pier. One is the forms that left visible marks on the outside; the other is the reinforcing steel bars that lie hidden below the surface. Each column is poured around a core of steel rebar that creates structural integrity by binding the column together from top to bottom from the inside out. Here we must observe that all analogies go only so far; they can only point, they cannot accurately replicate. Concrete columns are concrete columns; they are what they are for no other reason than that engineers and workmen have designed and constructed them to be what they are. Externally or internally the column has no choice.

But human being are not concrete pillars; they are creatures of life and choice. Therefore, their internal integrity is, in large degree, dependent upon individual choice. If the concrete pillars are poured around good steel rebar, the rebar will function with integrity because it has no choice; potentiality and actuality are one and the same. But, because human beings have the capacity to choose, our internal integrity is not axiomatic. The gap between our potentiality and our actuality we call sin; and the remedy we call grace through faith. And so, as surely as the columns of the Panama City Beach pier are held together by the external shape given them by the forms of the master engineer, and by the reinforcing steel inside each column, the Christian personality holds together because we are in the process of being shaped into the image of Jesus Christ; and because, "we walk by faith, not by sight" (II Cor. 5:7).

Reflection upon the Panama City Beach Fishing Pier reveals one final secret regarding its capacity to withstand the stormy gulf waters. When you walk under the pier you note that the columns don't all lean in the same direction. Some extend straight down from the underside of the pier and disappear into the sand. Others angle into the sand and water oriented on an east/west axis; yet others are angled on a north/south axis. What they have in common is the bedrock into which they are anchored at one end and the pier they support at the other. The end result is that the stresses sustained by the pier are distributed in 360 degree circles from the shore out into the gulf. Weight and stress are absorbed and dissipated evenly regardless of the direction from which the storm comes. Precisely because they are different, the supporting pillars are infinitely stronger and more effective in fulfilling their purpose than they would be if all were constructed in the same way. Oriented in the same direction each column would have to support one section of the pier independent of the others. Arranged the way they are, the pier columns support both the pier and one another simultaneously.

The Christian application is obvious. Christians share a common task; it is to support and participate in the purpose of God in the world expressed through the community of faith we call the church. To do so we must be deeply rooted in the bedrock of God's redemptive purpose. But commonly shared purpose and foundation must be complemented by individualized gifts and identity. To follow the analogy, we need enough commonality to be recognized as bridge supports; but our strength and effectiveness is enhanced, not weakened, by the fact that we do not all point in the same direction. What is important is that we are all rooted in the divine bedrock, and we are all united with the community of faith and its mission. Then, no matter which direction we lean (i.e., what our personal preferences, tastes, and idiosyncrasies happen to be) our distinctives are strengths, not weaknesses.

There is a personal application of this insight as well. Inevitably the storms of life will assail us, sometimes from various directions. If we try to maintain our stability in self-sufficient isolation we doom ourselves to failure. But when we lend our strength to others (all of whom are being buffeted as well) and they lend their strength to us, the likelihood of survival for all of us in enhanced immeasurably. It is our standing together in our diversity that prevents us from falling separately.

And so I looked at the old concrete fishing pier. Is it battered and scarred? Certainly. Is it still standing and fulfilling its purpose? Yes, indeed! Why? Because it is deeply grounded in its foundation. Because it is made from a substance that endures. Because it is carefully formed from the outside, and held together by steel rebar from the inside. And because its supporting pillars, though each is individual, all work together to achieve a common purpose.

Are we often battered and scarred? Certainly. Can we stand firm and fulfill our purpose? Yes, indeed! Why? Because we are deeply grounded in the purposes of God. Because we are a unique combination of the qualities of the God who made us, and the material substance of the universe around us. Because we are being shaped in the form of Christ-likeness, and we are held together internally by faith. And because each of us has been gifted with unique abilities that enable us to support one another in the achievement of a common purpose.

CHAPTER TWENTY-TWO
My Mother, the Philosopher

Though I was his welcome guest, I sat in the man's office in utter awe and terror. The massive desk between us was the most imposing piece of furniture I had ever seen. The walls were lined floor to ceiling with bookcases filled with volumes covering every subject imaginable. Though forty years have passed, I have no difficulty conjuring up a scene that marked a turning point in my life.

The man's name was Dr. David Mathews. At the time of our meeting he was Dean of Men at the University of Alabama. Some years later he became president of that institution only to resign to accept a cabinet post in the administration of President Gerald R. Ford. But all that lay ahead the day a fifteen- year old high school sophomore was his guest. I had been brought to meet Dr. Matthews by my high school biology teacher; a man who had taken an interest in my intellectual development, and who was attempting to steer me toward the University of Alabama as my choice of undergraduate schools.

Though obviously a busy man, Dr. Matthews chatted amiably with me asking questions about my academic interests. Wanting to impress the great man, I mumbled something about having recently become interested in philosophy. This immediately led to follow-up questions about whom I had been reading and what I thought about their ideas. It was apparent in seconds that I was in way over my head. But the man didn't humiliate me. Instead, he offered words of encouragement and said I should keep reading, even if I didn't fully understand what I read.

When it came time to leave, Dr. Matthews stepped from behind his desk and turned to a nearby bookcase. He pulled down a volume and handed it to me. It was a collection of the *Dialogues of Plato*. He said it was his gift to me, and he hoped one day I would study philosophy, if not at Alabama, then somewhere. I have seen the man only one time since that day, but I will always be grateful for his gracious hospitality. And the volume of Plato, even after forty years, remains one of my most treasured possessions.

Now I hold a PhD in the academic disciplines of Theology and Philosophy. I have taught in the field for two decades. I have read the works of some of the greatest minds in the history of Western Civilization. I have studied with outstanding teachers in some of the country's finest educational institutions. But, after all those years, and all that study, and all that teaching, the most influential philosophical mind I have encountered was that of "My Mother, the Philosopher."

In December, 1997, my mother suffered a massive stroke leaving her completely paralyzed on one side, partially paralyzed on the other, and unable to speak. Subsequent mini-strokes and seizures have been increasingly debilitating and now, when I go to see her, I often only discern a faint glimmer of the sharp, incisive mind that once glowed behind her eyes. But most of the things I have learned from the great intellects of Western Civilization have only been repetition and clarification of the foundational truths I first learned from her.

Make no mistaken assumptions about my mother. She never graduated from high school. She was not widely read or traveled. She had no formal training in the philosophical disciplines. Of the seventy-four years of her life prior to the stroke, she spent less than two of those years outside the west Alabama county in which she was born. But, she studied assiduously in the University of Life. And because of her willingness to learn and grow, my mother became wise. If the most simple definition of Philosophy is "love of wisdom," my mother was indeed a philosopher who though as deeply, and taught as truly, as anyone I have ever encountered.

Today I would share with you some of the remarkable truths I learned from this truly remarkable woman. One of the first life lessons I learned from my mother was to assume responsibility for my decisions, and my life. In difficult times she would say, "This is my canoe; and I'll paddle it the best I can." I could fill pages with the hardships and misfortunes of my mother's life, but never once have I heard her attempt to shift blame or responsibility away from herself and onto others. She taught me that, in the good times, it was her life; and, in the bad times, it was still her life.

Second, my mother taught me the importance of respecting myself if I expected to receive the respect of others. Socrates said, "Know thyself." My mother said, "You're not a nobody unless you think you are." Had my mother ever read her, she would have taken issue with Emily Dickinson's:

> *I'm nobody. Who are you?*
> *Are you nobody too?*

Long before I learned it from the biblical text, my mother taught me that I am "somebody" not "something," and no one can rob me of my "personhood" unless I permit them to. And respect for one's self is at the core of personhood.

A third profound truth my mother taught me was, "If you mess it up the first time, start over. And if you mess it up again, start over again." My students are often astounded when I tell them I flunked out of college four times before I ever successfully completed an academic semester. My problem was I was so afraid of "messing it up" that I inevitably did "mess it up" by giving up instead of seeing it through. My mother taught me there is a vast difference between "I didn't." and "I can't." Too often we conclude that "we can't" simply because "we didn't" the first, or second, or third time we tried. One success has a remarkable way of compensating for many, many failures.

I learned from my mother there is no amount of grief or hardship you can't transcend if you don't despair. Prior to her stroke at the age of seventy-four my mother had gone through a physically and emotionally abusive sixteen year marriage that ended in a terrible divorce. She buried two husbands and three sons, nearly lost me to a viral infection, and one of my sisters to a venomous spider bite. And she underwent half a dozen major surgical procedures. Instead of becoming cynical and embittered by such suffering, my mother could light up a room with her smile, and she embraced new friends and new experiences with zest and hopefulness.

Mother modeled for me the importance of allowing other people to be themselves, and to follow their own paths in life. Circumstances required that I leave home and begin to support myself at age sixteen.

Career and professional responsibilities have kept me away from my birth family and home town most of my adult life. Through all this separation my mother never once said, "When are you coming back home to live?" or "Why don't we see you more often?" or "If you loved us you wouldn't live so far away?" While she probably never read the verses, she understood the truth enshrined in Ada Roe's poem *Hearts:*

> *You cannot hope with hoops of steel*
> *To bind the questing heart.*
> *The heart must go adventuring*
> *In many a varied mart.*
>
> *The heart must go adventuring*
> *Along a lonely way.*
> *But it will still be coming home*
> *At closing of the day.*
>
> *The heart will still be coming home*
> *If it is free to stay.*
> *But hearts held close with hoops of steel*
> *May choose to stay away.*

I think I could have gone to my mother and said, "Mom, I'm going to the moon tomorrow." and she would have replied, "I love you son. Be careful, and come see me when you get back." She understood that my path was not the same as that of my brothers and sisters, and was wise enough to encourage me to follow it wherever it led.

While my mother was not traditionally religious, she often had profound religious insights. She taught me, before I ever discovered the Apostle Paul, that "if you don't have faith in yourself, you won't have faith in God either." Paul teaches that while none are "worthy of salvation" (Rom. 1:32, 2:1), God, in and through Jesus Christ, has judged each of us "worth" saving (Rom. 5:8-9, 10:9-10). There is a vast difference between run-a-way egoism and an appropriate sense of self-worth. Valuing ourselves and understanding our value to God are so closely connected that we separate them at our peril. Paul says, "I can do everything through him who gives me strength" (Phil. 4:13 NIV).

One of mother's favorite pass-times was playing dominoes. Over the years, visits home became opportunities for an evening or two of play with other family members. Mother and I were always partners, and we almost always won. When I was a child she taught me, "If you're gonna play dominoes, learn to count the spots." Anyone who plays knows that it isn't enough to know what "spots" you've got in your own hand; you've got to know what "spots" the others are holding as well. If you don't learn to "count the spots" you're going to get beaten every time. I don't know that Jesus ever played anything like dominoes, but he understood the concept of "counting spots": *Which of you, intending to build a tower, sitteth not down first, and counteth the cost, whether he have sufficient to finish it? Lest haply, after he hath laid the foundation, and is not able to finish it, all that behold it begin to mock him* (Lk. 14:28-29). One of my favorite sermon collections is Dr. C. Roy Angell's *The Price Tags of Life*. This former pastor of First Baptist Church, Miami, FL makes the point that while we are saved by the grace of God which is free (Eph. 2:8-9), everything in Christian growth and maturity has cost associated with it. Many believers fail to grow because they never learn to "count the spots" and reckon the cost in discipline, sacrifice, and just plain hard work.

One scene from childhood is impressed indelibly upon my memory. My older brother had crossed a pasture fence opposite our house to play. My mother, who at the time was heavily pregnant, sat on the front porch to keep an eye on me in the yard, and on my brother across the road in the pasture. Doug wandered too deeply into the pasture and attracted the attention of an irritable bull. After eying the boy menacingly, the beast lowered his massive head and charged. Doug began to run toward the fence, yelling at the top of his lungs, "Help, mother, help!" The distance was too great, her pregnancy was too inhibiting. All mother could do was yell in reply, "Run, Doug, run!" It seemed an eternity before my brother slid under the barbed-wire fence to safety, and all the while my ears rang with the dual cries, "Help, mother, help!" and "Run, Doug, run!" That day I learned, if you can't do anything else for someone in trouble, you can still encourage them.

Finally, for the sake of this little reflective exercise, there is one more truth to explore. Mother got involved in stuff. She was active in the PTA when we kids were in school. When the road through our rural community needed paving, she lobbied the County Commission until the job was finally done. When petitions were being circulated to install a water system, she collected more signatures than anyone. Throughout my childhood she was "president of this" and "chairman of that." She said, "If you don't like the way things are going, become the leader." Too many of us prefer to grouse, and complain, and whine rather than lead. We prefer the safety of the stands, or the pews of our churches, where we can cheer or jeer as the mood hits, but where we never have to take any personal risks. But, if I may change the metaphor, my mother taught me that you never hit home runs unless you step up to the plate and swing at the ball.

One of the most frequently quoted aphorisms of Abraham Lincoln is his observation, "All I am and ever hope to be I owe to my angel mother." While deeply grateful for the truths I have learned from the likes of Plato, Aristotle, Paul, Augustine of Hippo, Rene Descartes, Immanuel Kant, and dozens of others, I am most profoundly grateful for the lessons I learned from My Mother, the Philosopher.

CHAPTER TWENTY-THREE
Jesus Ain't Elvis, and Heaven Ain't Graceland in the Sky

One of the richest blessings, and one of the greatest dangers, in human understanding involves language. While modern science suggests that other animals make use of auditory symbols to communicate, none have the elaborate and complex systems of auditory symbols found in human languages. Contrary to the opinion of Dr. Doolittle, there is a profound difference between how human beings use language, and the way other animals use their linguistic symbol systems. And the difference is the human use of analogy.

By definition, an analogy is the comparison of one thing with another, one idea with another, one experience with another in order to distinguish how they are alike and how they differ. Through the use of analogy, we are able to move language beyond the concrete description of information reported by our senses and imagine things, or ideas, or events beyond the realm of our personal experience. Thus ancient humans, who had seen both horses and rhinoceroses, could, through the use of analogy, imagine the existence of mythical unicorns. Ancient philosopher/mathematicians whose eyes and hands reported to them the existence of flat surfaces, rounded surfaces, three-dimensional objects, etc. could, by analogy, infer the abstract geometric concepts of planes, circles, cubes, and spheres. This capacity of language to point, by analogy, beyond the finite and known, toward the infinite and unknown, enabled human beings to reflect upon the possibility that there was One like them, yet utterly different from them, who lay behind all that exists, and whose being gives meaning and purpose to the existence of everything else. At this point humans had begun to talk theologically. And all theological talk, all

"God talk," is analogical, for the best our language can do is point in the direction of the truth we wish to affirm.

And this is where the great challenge lies. Because we need to compare and contrast things, ideas, and experiences with one another in order to understand them; we often also collapse things, ideas, and experiences into one another and, thereby, lose the ability to distinguish them. It happens in a variety of ways. Sometimes our senses fool us. I recall having a friend visit at home one afternoon after school. I had been to his house many times, and his mother kept a bowl of fresh fruit on the kitchen table as a snack for my pal, his sister, and their friends. My mother kept a bowl of very real looking artificial fruit on our kitchen table that served no purpose except that of a decorative centerpiece. Unfortunately, my friend, assuming that fruit on the table at his house and fruit on the table at my house meant the same thing, grabbed a shiny apple and bit into it. What he got was not a chunk of red delicious, but a broken tooth.

Sometimes ideas do not transfer very well from one time period or cultural situation to another. When I teach world religions I point out that one way of categorizing religions is by their capacity to be examined systematically. The classical monotheisms of Western religious consciousness, (i.e., Judaism, Christianity, Islam, and to some degree, Zoroastrianism), lend themselves readily to systematic analysis. We can explore what the adherents of each religion believe about God, humankind, the origin and nature of the universe, salvation, scripture, eternal hope, etc. But one finds one's self in hopeless confusion if one attempts to superimpose this systematic schema upon Hinduism, Buddhism, or the various primal religions of Melanesia or sub-Saharan Africa. In fact, the meaning of ideas like God, salvation, heaven, and scripture may be very different from one religion to another; and may not even apply in some religions. Occasionally I hear someone express their religious tolerance by saying, "Well, I don't think it's really all that important which religion you follow. After all, we're all trying to get to the same place aren't we?" Obviously such a person doesn't know much about religions other than his/or her own; and, for that matter, they may not know much about the religion they claim as their own.

Sometimes our experiences fool us. This frequently happens when we transfer our feelings or impressions regarding one person to another person simply because they look, or act, or believe similarly. Thus the woman who has been raped may assume that every man who looks at her admiringly is a potential rapist. Or someone assumes that if one Palestinian is a suicide bomber, all Palestinians must be suicide bombers. Or another concludes that because they encountered one person in a particular profession who turned out to be a rascal, everyone in that profession must be a rascal as well.

The psychologists call this phenomenon projection and/or transference. We must think analogically in order communicate and understand. But when we fail to recognize what we are doing, or we do not think analogically with care, we often project or transfer our appropriate expectations of one person onto another for whom those expectations are inappropriate. We are particularly susceptible to this mistake in the area of religious expectations. We confuse what we might legitimately expect from one person, situation, or hope onto another person, situation, or hope. The end result is distortion, misunderstanding, and sometimes, just plain false conclusions. It is in this context that I suggest there are many in our contemporary religious environment who need to learn that "Jesus ain't Elvis; and heaven ain't Graceland in the sky."

Now, before you get ticked off because you think I've taken a shot at a cultural icon, let me affirm that I am a "baby boomer" born smack dab in the middle of the boom. Elvis and my older brother were in the Air Force in Germany at the same time, stationed on the same base. The feet propped on my desk while I write this are wearing penny loafers; and I combed my hair in a slicked back duck-tail until so much of it fell out I had to concede defeat and comb it another way. All I'm saying is that "Elvis was Elvis," and "Jesus is Jesus" and we should take care not to mistake one for the other. Both have offered us something, but what they have offered is not the same thing. And, consequently, what we owe to each of them is not the same thing either.

When we look at the two through the lens of analogy, there are ways we can certainly say they are alike. Both Jesus and Elvis were unlikely to amount to much by the success standards of their day. In many ways Tupelo, MS in the 1940's and 1950's and Nazareth in the first century A.D. paralleled one another. Nathanael Bartholomew was quoting a common proverb of the day when, in response to being told about Jesus, he said, "Can there any good thing come out of Nazareth?" (Jn. 1:46 KJV). No one expected much of anyone from Tupelo, MS either.

Both Jesus and Elvis broke with the cultural stereotypes of their day. Jesus refused to fit into the rigid ritualistic expectations of first century Pharisaic Judaism. And Elvis, breaking with the accepted musical canons of his time, synthesized musical forms from Negro Spirituals, Southern Gospel, Jazz, Country, and Blues into a unique blend others imitated, but that belonged to him alone.

Each connected the spiritual and the sensual aspects of human existence in ways that made the religiously pious uncomfortable. Jesus was accused of gluttony and drunkenness. And Elvis' famous gyrating pelvis was reviled in pulpits across the land. But there is significant similarity between the deep lessons of the parables of Jesus and the insights in such Elvis standards as *Love Me Tender, Heartbreak Hotel, Crying in the Chapel,* and *In the Ghetto.*

But, once all this has been acknowledged, we must remember that similarities do not equate to sameness. Elvis gave us the classic story of the unlikely kid who made good, beyond anyone's wildest expectations, in spite of the fact that all the cards were stacked against him. Elvis was a fantastic showman who gave every ticket holder his/her money's worth, and then some, with every performance. Elvis bought a palatial mansion outside Memphis for himself and his mama. From there they thumbed their noses at the rich, successful, snobbish southern culture that had dismissed them as "poor white trash" destined never to amount to much. For these reasons, among others, Elvis came to be "idolized."

So much for the Elvis myth, and our expectations of this cultural icon. The problem is that often people confuse their adulation of Elvis with their adoration of the God who created them, and who has redemptively revealed Himself in Jesus Christ. This is particularly evident in much contemporary media driven, and media imitating, worship. Elvis made us feel good, and we want Jesus to make us feel good too. Elvis was pretty, and we want everything about Jesus to be pretty. Elvis entertained us, and we want Jesus to entertain us too. Elvis took our minds off our problems, and we want Jesus to distract us as well. Elvis charmed us with his humble, "Thank you. Thank you very much," and we want Jesus to be a nice, down-home, well-mannered country boy from TBS's "My South." We don't really mind if Jesus is a little irreverent and satirical, as long as, Elvis and Jeff Foxworthy-like, he is soft-spoken, ironic, and doesn't really mean any harm.

But a careful look at the New Testament reveals a thoroughly different Jesus. It presents us with a Jesus who calls peremptorily, who confronts directly, who challenges openly, and who disturbs the complacency of the "up and out" and the "down and out" as well. He labeled the politically opportunistic Herod Antipas, "a fox" (Lk. 13:32), called upon the thrill-seeking inhabitants of Bethsaida and Chorazin to repent in sackcloth and ashes (Lk. 10:13), and denounced the self-satisfied Pharisees as "whited sepulchres . . . full of dead men's bones . . ." (Mt. 23:27). This Jesus is not depicted in the "paint on velvet" murals sold by vendors who will sell you one of Jesus, or sell you one of Elvis, or sell you one of each. We loved Elvis because he helped us escape from the humdrum ordinariness of our lives, made us forget for a time the consequences of our choices, and allowed us to live vicariously the life of sequined glitz, glamour, and gratuitous self-indulgence that he lived. Jesus demands that we live in the world, not escape from it. Jesus reminds us that there is no avoiding the consequences of our choices. And Jesus asserts that any vicarious identification with Him is expressed in the words: *If any man will come after me, let him deny himself, and take up his cross, and follow me. For whosoever will save his life shall lose it: and whosoever will lose his life for my sake shall find it* (Mt. 16:24 – 25). Nope, there's no doubt about it, "Jesus ain't Elvis."

And it's also true that "heaven ain't Graceland in the sky." I grew up just like you did singing, "I've got a mansion just over the hilltop . . . ." The image is drawn from the words of Jesus in John 14:2, "in my Father's house are many mansions" (KJV). Unfortunately, this is a place where the King James translators made a poor choice of English words to render the Greek. The Greek text reads *en te oikia tou patros mou monai pollai eisin* (literally, "in the house of my father there are many abiding places"). The vocal similarity between the Greek word *monai* and the Norman-English word *mansion* led to confusion. Interestingly enough, in John 14:23 they translated the same word, *monen,* correctly as *abode,* or "living place." Without doubt, Jesus is talking about heaven in John 14:2. But heaven is about living together with one another, and with the Father, in the Father's House, not in a place of our own. Heaven is not our own personal, private estate in the image of the 17th century manor house of English nobility. Nor is heaven a spiritualized version of Scarlett O'Hara's *Tara,* the *Biltmore House*, Elvis's *Graceland*, and certainly not Michael Jackson's *Neverland*.

What then is heaven? Heaven is where God's will is done (Mt. 6:10). Heaven is where the resurrected Christ sits at the right hand of God (Eph. 1:20). Heaven is where the resurrected redeemed sit together in Christ Jesus (Eph. 2:6). Heaven is that unmediated, uninterrupted, unqualified communion with God *where the tabernacle of God is with men, and he will dwell with them, and they shall be his people, and God himself shall be with them, and be their God. And God shall wipe away all tears from their eyes; and there shall be no more death, neither sorrow, nor crying, neither shall there be any more pain: for the former things are passed away* (Rev. 21:3 – 4 KJV). In a choice between John the Revelator's vision of heaven, and "Graceland in the Sky" I'll take John's vision every time. I don't want a "mansion just over the hilltop"; I want to live in the Father's house.

My friends, not only has Elvis left the building, he is also not coming back to receive his own unto himself, that where he is, there they may be also (Jn. 14:3). But, Jesus is!

CHAPTER TWENTY-FOUR
When the Emperor is Naked, Should You Say So?

Do you remember Hans Christian Andersen's wonderful story, *The Emperor's New Clothes*? In his vanity the emperor allowed himself to be duped by dishonest tailors who promised they could make him an outfit that would be invisible to all but those who were the most loyal and insightful. After many days passed, and much money was spent, the dishonest tailors pretended to clothe the emperor in garments that, in fact, were non-existent.

When the emperor paraded out before his subjects, not wishing to appear disloyal and/or stupid, the crowd "ooed" and "aahed" and made erudite remarks about the craftsmanship, quality, and beauty of the emperor's new clothes. Finally, a small boy, puzzled by the cognitive dissonance of the scene, shouted above the admiring voices, "But the emperor is naked!"

This public statement of what all present knew to really be true shocked everyone back to reality. There was just no "covering up" the fact that the emperor was naked.

Have you noticed how easy it is to be critical of those in positions of authority and responsibility? It matters not where the leadership is exercised: politics, business, education, religion, volunteer organizations, etc. Those persons who are willing to assume the mantel of leadership can be sure they will experience some measure of criticism. Someone is always willing to point out when the emperor/leader is naked (i.e., vulnerable, flawed, mistaken, wrong, etc.). There are both positives and negatives associated with this reality.

One positive quality has to do with the fact that we live in a free society where, short of libel and defamation of character, it is possible for us to express our opinions openly and honestly. One who has never experienced what it is like to live in a country where freedom of expression is curtailed, may fail to appreciate what a wonderful privilege the American freedom to "speak our minds" is.

Unfortunately, this freedom of expression is all too often exercised only about that with which we are dissatisfied, unhappy, or down right angry. And, all to often, we project our dissatisfaction, unhappiness, and anger about things onto the persons we consider responsible in the form of negative criticism. Most of us need to cultivate the habit of expressing our opinions about those things and persons with whom we are pleased, as well.

A second positive aspect of our capacity to criticize our leaders involves the possibility that leaders are afforded the opportunity to acquire a heightened consciousness of their accountability to others for the quality of leadership they provide. Sometimes leaders become detached from their constituencies in ways that militate against the best interests of all involved. Often such detachment requires that the leader be drawn back to reality by being reminded that others have voices, and opinions, and insights as well, and are not unwilling to express them. Dictators and tyrants may intimidate and coerce people into following them. But authentic leaders lead by the consent of those who are being led.

A third constructive possibility in criticism is its usefulness as a corrective for inappropriate behavior or muddled thinking. Over the years I have regularly made time to put myself in situations where others, whose judgment and insight I respect, could evaluate and critique my work. Often students ask, "Dr. Gregg, why do you spend your summers taking graduate courses at this or that university? You already have a Ph.D."

My answer is always, "In my office by myself, all my ideas are good ideas." You see, it is only when I allow my ideas to be challenged by those of other thinking persons that I can test and correct them. I need both the sincere affirmation, and the sincere criticism, of others.

Finally, when I listen to the criticism of others, I almost always get new ideas and insights. I have never learned anything new from a person who always agreed with me. While some people may grouse and complain just for the sake of hearing themselves make noise, this is not universally true. More often than not, the person who offers criticism has seen something that I missed, understands something I don't, or wishes to warn me of a danger I do not perceive. If I only engage the people who agree with me, I never encounter anything new. I just look at myself in the mirror and admire my own reflection. Some of my best ideas have been the by-product of being forced to listen to the critique of persons who disagreed, sometimes quite disagreeably, with me.

It is now time to return to the original question: "If the emperor is naked, should you say so?" Given my previous observations, it is clear that I think this question should be answered in the affirmative. Having said this however, I must move on quickly to assert that appropriate attention needs to be given to how one voices criticism. The truth is that the way criticism is expressed often neutralizes any possibility it has for making a constructive contribution in human relationships and problem solving. With this in mind, there are a number of suggestions worth considering regarding the appropriate way to offer critical guidance to our leaders, or "to tell the emperor that he/she is naked."

First, and perhaps foremost, one should genuinely care about the well- being and success of the person about, or to whom, criticism is being offered. Otherwise, our critiques may be no more than expressions of envy, dislike, or prejudice. That which motivates our criticism is an important factor to be considered. Remember, there is no such thing as a totally objective and unbiased opinion. The very fact that we have an opinion reflects that we are sufficiently invested in the issue to care how it is resolved. If our motivation for offering criticism is inappropriate, this is likely to be perceived by others, and may do considerably more harm than good. I think it was this reality Jesus had in mind when he cautioned the excessively critical of his day: "Why do you look at the speck of sawdust in your brother's eye and pay no attention to the plank in your own eye? (Mt. 7:3 NIV). If your reason for telling the emperor that he is naked is to embarrass or demean, injure or offend, it is usually just as well left unsaid. Without genuine care for the best interest of the other, critical feedback quickly descends into petty fault finding.

Second, if we must criticize, we should do more than vent vague dissatisfaction. Be specific. Too often criticism is expressed in the voice of Puddle Glum from C.S. Lewis' *The Chronicles of Narnia*. Puddle

Glum never saw anything in a positive light, and was sure the worst was always going to happen. If something troubles us enough to talk about it publicly, we should be sufficiently focused to be specific about our concern. Leaders aren't helped by vague, unfocused, often whining expressions of discontent. After a time, if we regularly express our concerns in this way, we find, more often than not, we are dismissed with the observation, "So and so gets his/her kicks out of being negative."

Third, any criticism or critique we have for our leaders should be offered directly, and preferably, privately. Rarely is anything worthwhile ever accomplished by trying to talk to one person through another person. Vague statements such as, "Some people are saying," or "I have heard a number of people say" aren't especially helpful because, all too often, we are simply putting our own words in other people's mouths. And, in many instances, the reason "other" people have been talking is that "we" have been going around bringing up the subject. Integrity insists that we have the courage to speak our own minds directly. Hiding behind the anonymous voices of others is a form of moral cowardice.

Akin to this is another behavior that is universally destructive. Among the greatest impediments to positive human relationships is the appearance we often present of double-mindedness. This is evident when we appear to agree in one setting and then voice our dissent in another. It is a terrible betrayal to permit a leader to think you are in agreement with him/her, only to have the leader find out later that you aren't. It is exceedingly difficult to trust again if you have ever gone out on a limb, thinking someone was behind you, only to look back and discover that the person you trusted is sawing off the limb.

The most effective and helpful communication is that which takes place when, in an appropriate setting, we speak our minds, and speak with our own voices, rather than borrowing the voices of others. And remember, James says, "A double-minded man is unstable in all his ways" (James 1:7 KJV). While James doesn't say so directly, double-minded women are equally unstable.

Fourth, whenever possible some word of affirmation should be offered along with our criticism. Rarely is someone always wrong, mistaken, inept, or incompetent. Most leaders, particularly those within volunteer settings, want to serve effectively and make a positive difference in the world. Criticism and verbal abuse are not the same thing. People need to be told what they are getting "right" as well as what they are getting "wrong." The ancient sage of Israel was correct when he said,

A word aptly spoken is like apples of gold in settings of silver.
Like an earring of gold or an ornament of fine gold
is a wise man's rebuke to a listening ear.
Like the coolness of snow at harvest time
is a trustworthy messenger . . . . (Prov. 25:11-13a)

While negative criticism is sometimes useful for correction and instruction, it is positive affirmation that motivates people who are striving to improve themselves.

A fifth aspect of the manner in which criticism is offered relates to our willingness to suggest alternative approaches to the circumstances that concern us. Almost anyone can point out when something is broken. It is something else to offer helpful suggestions regarding how something broken can be fixed.

All too often we want to point out what is wrong and then, when someone asks what we would do differently, we say, "That's not my problem." When this happens our criticism turns out to be little more than an indication of our willingness to take "cheap shots" at people who are already wounded. Sometimes, when we say, "that won't work," we are really saying, "I don't want it to work."

Lastly, those who are reluctant to become involved in fixing the problems should be sparing in their criticism of others. If you don't like what's happening in your church, or PTO, or civic club go beyond vocalizing that which you don't like by making yourself available to be a part of the solution. Many of us are like the bystander at a house fire who, while standing on the hose, criticized the firemen for not being able to get enough water on the flames.

Don't play the silly game of saying, "I could help solve that problem if she/he would ask me?" Don't allow pride and ego to seduce you into contributing to the failure of another when all that is needed for success is your willingness to help. To deliberately withhold needed help and support you are capable of providing exhibits an attitude of self-centered mean-spiritedness that does no one any good, and often does great harm.

From time to time every leader, like the gullible emperor in Hans

Christian Andersen's story, is going to be found naked (i.e., inadequate, unprepared, mistaken, wrong). Those who lead us are subject to the same human foibles as are we. For that reason they need, appropriately given, our criticism and critique. But they don't need our undifferentiated frustration, dissatisfaction, and anger dumped on them simply because they are easy to unload on. The observation has been made that the difference between a "pat on the back" and a "kick in the pants" is about eighteen inches. From time to time all of us need some of both. But how each is delivered is at least as important as the "kick" or the "pat."

CHAPTER TWENTY-FIVE
What If You Are the Naked Emperor?

In the preceding essay I made use of Hans Christian Andersen's time-less tale, *The Emperor's New Clothes,* as a vehicle for reflection upon the method and manner by which we offer criticism to those who lead us. That reflection looked through the eyes of the little boy who pointed out the emperor's nakedness. It seems useful to explore the same circumstances from the perspective of the naked emperor. How does one, particularly someone who leads others, respond when the world is suddenly confronted with the reality of his/her "nakedness"? Or, put more bluntly, what do we do when it becomes evident that we are the naked emperor? Our response, in many was, both demonstrates the authenticity of our personhood, and determines the effectiveness of our ability to lead in the future.

An adequate response to "nakedness" begins with the realization and acceptance of the reality that all persons have vulnerabilities ("naked" places). One of the most difficult of human realities is the acknowledg-ment of one's own "nakedness." With every fiber of our being we strive to deny Job's confession, "Naked I came from my mother's womb, and naked I will depart" (Job 1:21 NIV). When one reflects on the matter, it is remarkable how much time and energy each of us devotes to making sure we are "covered." We want enough income to "cover" our financial obligations. At least annually most of us review our automobile, homeowners, professional, health, and life insurance policies to be sure we are adequately "covered." Soldiers in an urban battlefield "cover" one another as they move from doorway to doorway and building to building. When we want to conceal our activities we often develop elaborate "cover" stories to account for our comings and goings. Yet, strive as we may, unexpected financial crises upset our budgets. Catastrophic illnesses, professional malfeasances, fires and floods, and such like inevitably reveal limitations, exclusions, and gaps in our efforts to "cover" ourselves against life's disasters. The hidden sniper or unpredictable event leads to violent death or humiliating embarrassment when our "cover" is blown and we are suddenly exposed.

Regardless of the effort, and certainly prudence dictates taking sensible precautions, we can never guarantee that someone or something will not reveal truths about us we would prefer the world never know. Our language is filled with quaint expressions acknowledging the inevitable revelation of our weaknesses, flaws, bad choices, misdemeanors, crimes: "feet of clay," "warts and all," "hand in the cookie jar," "held up to the light," "caught with our pants down," etc.

To a great degree, it is simply a matter of coming to grips with our personal humanity. Noble as is the human creature, we are not perfect. Environmentally we are thrown, physically we are weak, psychologically we are insecure, socially we are deviant, and theologically we are fallen. These truths are not troughs in which we should wallow; but they are also not trivialities to be dismissed as irrelevant. Only harm is to be done, to ourselves and others, by denying the reality of our human limitations. When we do so we impose expectations upon ourselves we cannot possibly meet. Further, we increase the likelihood of the exposure of the very things about ourselves we would most like to keep hidden. This delusion of ourselves, and denial of our humanity, makes it almost impossible for us to be genuinely transparent and honest with others. Relationships become games of psycho-social "hide-and-seek" as each tries to keep "covered" his or her own "nakedness" while exposing the "nakedness" of the other.

Genuine acceptance of the reality of one's humanity makes possible the realization that one cannot authentically lead others without risking the exposure of one's "nakedness." Leadership is about calculating risk and taking chances in order to achieve worthwhile objectives. There is no genuine success where there is no possibility of failure. Too often we confuse the realities of "I am naked" and "I am ashamed." In the biblical story of humankind's expulsion from the Garden of Eden, the man's confession highlights his confusion of "nakedness" and "shame." Thus Adam responds to the "Where are you?" of the Creator by hiding in fear and shame from face to face encounter with his Maker (Gen. 3:9-10). But there was no shame in Adam's nakedness. Both the man and the woman were unashamedly naked prior to partaking of the forbidden fruit. Adam should have been ashamed, not of his nakedness, but of his disobedience to the Divine command.

Often in our lives we express shame for our failures. But there is no shame in failure at the end of sincere and responsible striving. Shame is the product of not trying, or of trying inappropriately. Shame should be the consequence of knowing better and willfully not doing better. There is no shame in having done the best one can and still not succeed. All one can do is all one can do, and there is no shame in reaching the limit of one's ability or capacity.

It is here that the authentic leader is to be distinguished from the pseudo-leader. The pseudo-leader wants others to do the risking, while she reaps the benefits of the risks taken. The pseudo-leader strives to "cover" himself by shifting blame for failure onto others. The pseudo-leader has great difficulty in "owning" his limitations so that, in conjunction with others, he may move forward successfully. The pseudo-leader, with her "nakedness" exposed in ways that even a child can recognize, insists on strutting onward, pretending to be clothed in regal splendor. Unable or unwilling to hear the voices of others, the pseudo-leader listens only to those voices that echo his own.

In contrast, the authentic leader understands that integrity of personhood is the single most important quality in effective leadership. Integrity of personhood does not mean one is without flaws. Integrity of personhood means that one is self-aware enough of one's imperfections to not be drawn aside from the goal in vain efforts to deny or disguise one's limitations. Integrity of personhood makes it possible for the authentic leader to minimize her limitations by surrounding herself with others whose abilities supplement the weaknesses and limitations of the leader. A blind man has no need for another blind man to help him see; a deaf man has no need for another deaf man to help him hear. But if the blind man lends his ears to the sighted man, and the sighted man lends his eyes to the blind man, both profit from the partnership. Authentic leaders do not deny their need for others to clarify their vision, sharpen their hearing, and refine their judgment. An authentic leader recognizes the futility of attempting to "cover" one's nakedness. Rather, he trusts others who are equally naked, in different ways, and together they "cover" one another's "nakedness" (vulnerabilities) by sharing one another's strengths.

The primary question confronting today's leader is that of acknowledging one's vulnerabilities and limitations while continuing to exercise positive, effective leadership. In geometry, the term "congruence" refers to the relationship of objects or forms which, when superimposed on one another, correspond exactly. Or, put another way, "A" and "B" in congruence are identical to one another. In personality theory, congruence references the nearness of one's perception of one's being/behaving and one's actual being/behaving.

It seems that the best way for leaders to minimize the risks of becoming the naked emperor, or to be able to continue to lead effectively in the aftermath of having one's "nakedness" (vulnerability) exposed, consists of living in such a way that there is as near congruence as possible between the "self" we wish to disclose to the world and the actual "self" of our innermost being. This congruence of personhood expresses itself in two dimensions of our living: the public/private and the outer/inner.

By public/private is meant the moral/ethical expressions of our personhood. Often leaders risk exposing their "nakedness" by posing as paragons of public virtue and rectitude while, in their private lives, they indulge in behaviors that run diametrically contrary to the moral/ethical values they publicly espouse. One of the saddnesses of history is the multitude of names on the list of persons whose effectiveness was destroyed by the revelation of glaring inconsistencies between their public self and their private self. No vocation is immune from this tragedy. Political leaders, clergy, teachers, business persons, athletes, entertainers, law enforcement persons; this list goes on both *ad infinitum* and *ad nauseum*.

By inner/outer is meant the relationship between how we present ourselves to those around us and how we actually perceive, feel, and think. Often this is as simple as the tensions of introversion/extroversion in our lives. Personally, I struggle with being, in many ways, an introvert who prefers the quiet of his study, solitary reflection, and personal privacy. This often stands in stark contrast to my very public professional activities as vocational minister, college teacher, and free-lance writer. The maintenance of appropriate balance between these inner and outer expressions of life is sometimes difficult, but never a major life problem for

me. There are occasions, however, when persons have such great difficulty managing the balance between introversion and extroversion that it
leads to depression, bi-polarity, delusional behavior, and even suicide.

Likewise, in social relationships, there are those who outwardly
present themselves as tolerant, inclusive, accepting, and trustworthy.
Unfortunately, sometimes internally these persons are judgmental, harbor
strong prejudices, are contemptuous of others, or suffer from severe sexual
maladjustment. Behind a façade of conviviality there often lurks stark
racism, smoldering hatred, or a propensity toward violent, abusive behavior. Such radical disjunction between the inner self and the outer self is
often a source of great pain to the person and others with whom life must
be shared. For, sooner or later, some triggering event or experience will
expose this deep incongruity between the person's inner and outer self.
When this happens the consequence is often shattered lives, broken relationships, and, sometimes, even physical death.

By now it should be evident that on some occasion, and perhaps
on more than one, those of us who have sought, or been thrust, into positions of leadership have become painfully aware that our vulnerabilities
have been uncovered. The little boy has cried out as we passed by, "The
emperor is naked!" While we may posture and pretend for a time, ultimately we are forced to acknowledge what everyone else already knows,
"I am the naked emperor."

When this happens we have a number of options. We can delude
ourselves into thinking it isn't really true, and continue to march on, ignor-
ing the laughter and pity of those who line the path. We can scramble to
"cover" ourselves, shift the blame, and refuse to "own" the truth about
ourselves. We can seek to divert attention from our "nakedness" by exposing the "nakedness" of others.

These are all negative, and ultimately destructive, responses. There
are at least two better alternatives. First, before the nakedness is exposed, we can seek to maintain a fundamental congruence between our
public and our private selves, our inner and outer selves. By doing so,
when we come to places of leadership we will have been placed there by
persons who valued us as we genuinely are, as opposed to how they
thought us to be. Those who seek positions of leadership, for whatever
reasons, may find this approach particularly difficult because they are politically astute enough to understand that for most people "perception IS

148

reality." Consequently, many are seduced by the temptation to present themselves in ways assured to evoke the desired responses from others. But then the day comes when the façade is stripped away and naked truth becomes apparent to everyone.

The other positive alternative can be employed only after the "nakedness" (vulnerability) has been exposed. It involves, no matter how painful, the process of acknowledging the truth about ourselves and our actions. Without attempting to shrug it off, laugh it off, or minimize the truth in any other way, we simply say, "Now you know the truth. You may or may not think I still deserve to be your leader. You may not wish for me to continue to lead you. But, if you are willing to forgive, I am willing to learn and grow." There is no guarantee that others will respond with grace and forgiveness. Sometimes others are so fearful of the exposure of their own "nakedness" they cannot tolerate the exposed "nakedness" of another. But at least such a response is rooted in the choice to "own" the truth, rather than the continued perpetuation of a lie.

CHAPTER TWENTY-SIX
Descartes: I Think, Therefore I Am –
Gregg: I Am, Therefore I Think

In the 17th century a remarkable mind emerged in France. Rene Descartes, the son of an old and respected French family, decided to explore a method for arriving at absolute knowledge regarding the universe in which we live, and the reliability of any knowledge we possess. In his *Discourses on Method* Descartes describes his decision to systematically doubt the reality of everything his senses reported to him until he came to something he could not logically doubt. Using this approach of methodological doubt, Descartes doubted the information reported by his senses, doubted the findings of the natural sciences, doubted the reality of the material world, and doubted the existence of God. Finally Descartes came upon something whose existence he could not doubt: he was sure he could not logically doubt the reality of his own existence, because he could not doubt that he was, in fact, doubting. His conclusion is summarized in the famous dictum: *Cogito, Ergo Sum* – "I Think, Therefore I Am."

Descartes' radical rationalism emerged as a watershed in the history of the development of western philosophical reflection. Subsequent thinkers have agreed or disagreed with Descartes, but none have been able to ignore him. He established that one essential way of describing what it means for one to be human is to understand that we are we are "thinking things." While other animals may think, may even solve problems, human beings are the only creatures who appear to think about their thinking.

This is not the place to analyze and critique the strengths and weaknesses of Descartes method, nor to appraise the validity of his conclusions. Whether Descartes' conclusion, "I think, therefore I am" is valid or not, I am sure that because "I am" it is incumbent upon me to "think." Thus, the maxim by which I choose to live is, "I Am, Therefore I Think." I am a thinking reality as surely as I am a breathing reality, or a reproducing reality, or a psychological reality, or a spiritual reality. To exist, to be, is to think. About this I have no choice. What I may choose is that about which I elect to think, and the clarity of the thinking I do. In order to do this, I need two things: The first is a disciplined key that focuses my mind on subject matter worthy of my thought. The second is a series of reliable principles to enable the avoidance of muddle-headedness and confusion. The question is, "Where does one begin?"

Some will recall that I frequently describe myself in Christian terms as a "believing thinker" and a "thinking believer." I am convinced that genuine Christian commitment requires both the embracing of certain foundational beliefs about God, humankind, and the universe in which we live; and careful examination of those beliefs and their logical consequences, making use of all the tools of human reason, scientific exploration, and rational reflection. Such an affirmation provides the "key" or beginning point of my thinking, and it is here that Descartes and I part company. The great French philosopher elected "doubt" as his point of beginning; I choose to begin with "faith." Descartes' motto was "I will believe nothing." Mine is, "I will believe something." Not "everything," but "something."

Now, before I proceed further, I must define authentic Christian faith. The Greek word from the New Testament is *pistis*, and it deserves defining as it was classically used, rather than as it has come to be popularly used today. This requires some discussion of what the term does not mean. Authentic Christian "faith" is not naïve credibility. Christian "faith" is not a blind leap. Christian "faith" is not Tertullian's assertion, "I believe because it is ridiculous." Christian "faith" is not a body of neatly packaged theological affirmations labeled "the Christian Faith." And genuine Christian "faith" is not a psychological crutch devised by neurotics as a coping mechanism to assist in managing the difficulties, and hardships, and sufferings of life.

If authentic Christian "faith" is not any of these, what then is it? What does the term "faith" genuinely mean? This is a legitimate question and it deserves a straight-forward answer. The word *pistis* was not coined by early Christians so that it has only a Christian definition. It was not even lifted from the common language and redefined to give it an exclusively Christian meaning. Rather, it was used by biblical writers in much the same way it was used in the larger culture of the 1ˢᵗ century A.D. Because this is true, an examination of how the word was used in Greco-Roman culture will yield insight into its New Testament meaning.

One writer has asserted that in the Greco-Roman world *pistis* primarily meant "firm persuasion, a conviction based upon hearing" (Vine, *An Expository Dictionary of New Testament Words*, Vol. 2, p. 71). The outstanding Greek scholars, Gerhard Kittel and Gerhard Friedrich, define the term *pistis* as "confidence," "trust," "firm conviction," "dependable truth or knowledge" (Kittel and Friedrich, *Theological Dictionary of the New Testament,* Vol. 6, p. 176 – 177).

When one examines classical non-biblical literature, the New Testament, the early Church Fathers, and subsequent Christian thinkers, the consensus of definition is clear. From the Christian perspective, "faith" is an *epistemology*, a way of knowing certain kinds of truth. "Faith" is a way of knowing as surely as intuitive insight, instinctive reaction, rational reflection, empirical investigation, and sensory experience are ways of knowing. We cannot answer every question with the knowledge accessible through faith any more than we can answer every question through one of these other ways of knowing. That's why I don't have much use for bumper stickers that say, "Jesus is the answer." If the question is, "What is the sum of 2 plus 2?" Jesus is not the answer. If the question is, "How far is it from the earth to the moon?" Jesus is not the answer. If the question is, "Should I get immediate medical attention if I am struck by a rattlesnake?" Jesus is not the answer. The answers to these kinds of questions are found through rational reflection, scientific measurement, and reason based upon knowledge of what has happened to others who didn't get immediate medical attention after being bitten by rattlesnakes. Tools must be suited to tasks. "Faith" is not the only tool that should be in the Christian believer's bag; but no bag of tools for Christian living is complete that does not include biblical faith.

A second reason for my choice of "faith" as a starting point in contrast to Descartes' "doubt" is that "faith" and "doubt" are not opposites; they are close relatives. This is why all attempts to quantify faith in terms of "how much" or "how little" someone has are all nonsense. Faith

152

is not a commodity to be quantified in pounds, or yards, or gallons. Faith is a choice one either makes, or does not make. The choice of faith is not a categorical rejection of doubt; it is a deliberate choice one makes in the midst of one's doubting. Remember the man who said to Jesus, "Lord, I believe; help thou mine unbelief" (Mk. 9:24). Jesus did not rebuke the man; rather Jesus healed the man's son because of the sincerity of the faith expressed in spite of the doubt that was there as well. Faith is not the absence of doubt; faith is the courage to choose and act in spite of one's doubt.

Descartes chose to doubt until he came upon a reality it was logically impossible to doubt. I chose to believe until I am provided with sufficient reason to doubt. The difference is this. Descartes wanted absolute assurance and thought he had discovered it. Many in Descartes' day, and across the generations, have pointed out the weakness of Descartes, "I think, therefore I am." While the method of doubt may yield some truth, it does not yield absolute truth. Descartes would have been more accurate had he concluded, "I think I think, therefore I think I am."

My aim is more modest. I make no demands for absolute knowledge about anything. Such demands end in paralysis because the quest for absolute assurance makes it impossible to ever make a choice. I am content with "sufficient reason," for sufficient reason opens the way to genuine Christian faith while retaining the value of the corrective quality of doubt. You see, this Christian faith is risky business. And, by faith, I have elected to take the risk that "believing something" leads in a better direction than "doubting everything."

We have established the disciplined key needed to focus my mind on subject matter worthy of my thought. Remember, "I am," therefore I cannot "not" think. I can only make choices about the content of my thinking, and about the quality or precision of my thought. But, as long as "I am" I must think.

If authentic Christian faith is the disciplined key, what are some principles that will help me avoid muddle-headedness and confusion? In the scope of this reflection, every principle cannot be discussed in detail, but there are certain basic principles worthy of consideration.

The preceding discussion revealed that the assertion "I choose to believe" and the assertion "I choose to doubt" are both assertions of faith because neither can demonstrate its truth claims with absolute certainty. I affirm that the positive choice to "believe something" is a more reliable guide to clear thinking than the negative choice to "doubt everything." Radical skepticism leads to paranoid close-mindedness. There is no qualitative distinction between the man who says, "This is what I believe, and I don't want to talk about it" and the man who says, "I don't believe anything, and I don't want to talk about it." Both suffer from intellectual constipation. I frequently encourage students to make decisions that open doors rather than decisions that close doors for them. Thus my first guiding principle is the conviction that the choice to "believe" opens up more meaningful possibilities than the choice to radically "doubt."

A second guiding principle that helps avoid muddle-headedness and confusion is that of not being afraid of the truth wherever and however it is found. As a Christian, I believe that all genuine "truth" is ultimately and finally God's truth. And if all truth is God's truth, I have nothing to fear in the truth. Genuine truth is not confining and destructive; it is liberating and transforming. Remember, Jesus said, "You shall know the truth, and the truth shall set you free" (Jn. 8:32).

Third, there is the "flotsam and jetsam" principle. "Flotsam and jetsam" refer to the material one finds floating on the surface, or left on the beach, after a tidal surge. Here, I refer to that "stuff" that floats to the surface of one's mind when one is not consciously thinking about anything. It is an interesting, and sometimes scary, exercise to critically examine what one find's oneself thinking about when the mind is disengaged and drifting. What do you find yourself thinking about when you aren't really thinking about anything at all? Anger? Resentment? Envy? Pornography? Revenge? Greed? It is a wonderful thing that we cannot read one another's thoughts, for if we could we would be shocked and astounded by what we find. Some say, "You are what you eat." I suggest, "We are what we think."

The Apostle Paul understood the importance of training our minds so our thoughts reflect the Christian persons we wish to be. In Philippians 4:8 he counseled, *whatsoever things are true, whatsoever things are honest, whatsoever things are just, whatsoever things are pure, whatsoever things are lovely, whatsoever things are of good report; if there be any virtue, and if there be any praise, think on these things.* Some things are just not worth the time and energy it takes to think about them. Therefore, it is important that we develop the capacity to think

154

those thoughts most conductive to our positive Christian development. Real character is never imposed from the outside in; it always emerges from the inside out. Thus it is important that we train our minds to think about the genuinely important things: *truth, honesty, justice, purity, love, worthiness, virtue, praise.* Otherwise, we will find ourselves thinking about anything and everything.

Other principles could be mentioned; but these three are essential: 1) Open-ended faith in God. 2) Fearless trust in the truth wherever it is found. 3) And mental discipline that accepts responsibility for the content of one's thinking. "I Am, Therefore I Think!"

CONCLUSION

*L*et us hear the conclusion of the whole matter: Fear God, and keep his commandments: for this is the whole duty of man (Ecc. 12:13 KJV). All that has been asserted in this modest work is summarized in these words from Ecclesiastes. In the preceding pages a *believing thinker* and a *thinking believer* has made no attempt to be either profound or original. Rather, I have sought to be honestly reflective and openly confessional. If my musing upon the content and practice of the Christian faith has been helpful to you, I am grateful. If these exercises have aided in the honing of your own critical reflective skills, I have achieved my purpose. If you have discovered that "I honestly don't know, but I haven't given up on learning," is a legitimate Christian response to life's most difficult questions, you have joined a numberless company of believers from the Apostle Paul to the present. They were and are women and men committed to "love the Lord, [their] God with all [their] heart, and with all [their] mind . . ." (Mt. 22:37).

In a world that many are referring to as post-Christian, and perhaps even anti-Christian in its orientation, the context of contemporary Christianity is, in many ways, analogous to that of the 2nd and 3rd centuries of the Christian Era. This was the time of the great early Christian Apologists such as Ignatius of Antioch, Clement of Alexandria, Justin Martyr, Irenaeus of Lyon, and Origen of Caesarea. With passionate hearts and disciplined minds, these first Christian theologians stood firm against the sneering criticism, disparaging contempt, and hostile rejection of the Greco-Roman intellectual, political, and cultural environment of the early Church. In the face of ridicule, false accusation, and persecution, these early *believing thinkers and thinking believers* out thought, out taught, out loved, and out served the world in which they lived. Conditioned by their culture, frequently less than perfect in their understanding, and often blinded

155

by their own prejudices, they "saw through a glass darkly," but they still saw enough to change the world.

Today's world needs men and women who will stand on the shoulders of those who have gone before them, who will learn from their insights and their mistakes, and who will take up the task of doing for present and future generations what these early saints did for those long ago. The task is called *Apologetics*. Do not misunderstand the word; it has nothing to do with expressing sorrow, or remorse, or embarrassment for one's Christian convictions. Rather *Apologetics* is the discipline that takes seriously the injunction of I Peter 3:15 to *be ready always to give an answer to every man that asketh you a reason of the hope that is in you* . . . (I Peter 3:15 KJV).